10 01 01-042137 012   W9-CSI-544
MORRIS, JAN
TRAVELS
(1) 1976 910.4

CENTRAL   c. 1

        Morris, Jan, 1926-
910.4   Travels / Jan Morris ; with ill. by
        Nicholas Hall. 1st American ed. New York
        : Harcourt Brace Jovanovich, c1976.
        155 p. : ill. ;

        "A Helen and Kurt Wolff book."

                OFFICIAL
                DISCARD
        SONOMA COUNTY LIBRARY

        1.Voyages and travels-1951- -Collected
        works. 2.Travelers-Collected works.
        I.Title

        910'.4   G163.M67 1976
                                    76-2531

TRAVELS

BY THE SAME AUTHOR

AS I SAW THE U.S.A.

SULTAN IN OMAN

SOUTH AFRICAN WINTER

THE HASHEMITE KINGS

THE WORLD OF VENICE

THE ROAD TO HUDDERSFIELD

THE PRESENCE OF SPAIN
(*with Evelyn Hofer*)

CITIES

OXFORD

PAX BRITANNICA

THE GREAT PORT

PLACES

HEAVEN'S COMMAND

CONUNDRUM

910.4

JAN MORRIS

TRAVELS

With illustrations by Nicholas Hall

SONOMA CO. LIBRARY

A HELEN AND KURT WOLFF BOOK

HARCOURT BRACE JOVANOVICH

NEW YORK AND LONDON

Copyright © 1976 by Jan Morris

All rights reserved. No part of this publication
may be reproduced or transmitted in any form or
by any means, electronic or mechanical, including
photocopy, recording, or any information storage
and retrieval system, without permission in
writing from the publisher.

Printed in the United States of America

Library of Congress Cataloging in Publication Data

Morris, Jan, date
Travels.
"A Helen and Kurt Wolff book."
1. Voyages and travels—1951-   —Collected works.
2. Travelers—Collected works.   I. Title.
G163.M67 1976   910'.4   76-2531
ISBN 0-15-191075-8

First American edition

B C D E

For
HELEN WOLFF
and
CHARLES MONTEITH
with love, thanks
and apologies

CONTENTS

ACKNOWLEDGEMENTS

The essays on Ibn Batuta and William Hickey were first published in *Horizon*, New York, and those on Hong Kong and Singapore in *Encounter*, London. *The Times* of London first published the piece on Dublin and 'On the Confederation Special'. 'Through My Guide-Books' is from *The Times Literary Supplement*, London, 'On Wateri-ness' from the *Sunday Times*, London, the Washington essay from *Rolling Stone* of San Francisco, the essay on Edinburgh from *Diversions* of New York.

I am grateful to all their Editors and Proprietors for permission to republish now.

INTRODUCTORY

When I was small the only sermon I enjoyed, the only one indeed I really listened to, was the old familiar about Life as a Journey—the Mr. Christian sermon, the stony upland sermon, the best foot forward, cross-roads, far horizon sermon. Its imagery appealed to me from the start, for I realized myself already to be of the wandering kind.

Since then the parable has been proved for me. For one thing I have come to see my own life, however others see it, as a prolonged and fascinating quest. For another, believing as I now do implicitly in *after*-lives, I foresee no final destination. And for a third, hardly less telling, I have for twenty years and more made a happy living out of travelling—travelling in fact, travelling in fantasy, in present as in past.

So this small and eclectic collection of essays offers, so to speak, a frivolous rubric to that text. It reflects a sense of pilgrimage, it recognizes several dimensions to the experience of travel, and it expresses some of the endless pleasures I have gained from the chances of a travelling life. I do hope it does not bore you. Some people, I know, prefer the one about Life's Lottery.

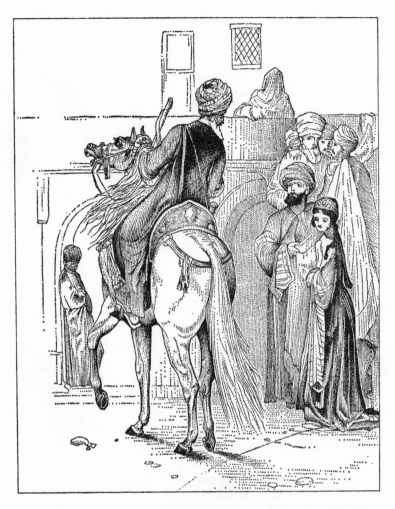

THE BEST TRAVELLED MAN IN THE
WORLD

One day in the Muslim year 756 (1355 in our chronology) a well-
known Moroccan theologian began to dictate his memoirs. His name
was Abu Abdullah Mohammed, better known by his patronymic
Ibn Batuta, and he was fifty-one years old. Since he was committing
his memories to paper under instructions from the Commander of the

Faithful, the Sultan Abu Inan Faris of Morocco, he began them
ritually:

> *In the Name of God the Merciful, the Compassionate: Praise be to
> God, Who hath subdued the earth to His servants that they may tread
> thereon spacious ways, Who hath made therefrom and thereunto the
> three moments of growth, return and recall, and hath perfected His
> Bounty towards His creatures in subjecting to them the beasts of the
> field and vessels towering like mountains, that they may bestride the
> ridge of the wilderness and the deeps of the ocean.*

The imagery of this dedication was more than figurative. Though
Ibn Batuta was a scholar and a distinguished *qadi*, or judge, he was
chiefly known as a traveller. He was not merely well travelled by
Moroccan standards: he was the best travelled man on earth, and had
probably seen more of the world than anybody else ever had. By sea
and by land, on foot, by camel and on horseback, he had travelled at
least 75,000 miles, a total probably never equalled by one man until
the age of steam. He was unique. He, and probably he alone among all
the men of his age, had visited every civilized country there was.

* * *

Civilization, of course, lies in the eye of the beholder, but to the
Sultan Abu Inan Faris, to Ibn Batuta himself, and to any educated
citizen of fourteenth-century Morocco, it was coterminous with
Islam. It was 600 years since the Arabs, bursting from their desert
heartlands, had carried their austere and warlike faith across the
continents, and by the fourteenth century the great Islamic Empire of
the Caliphs was no more, having split into a multitude of sultanates,
amirates and squabbling principalities. It remained nevertheless, if not
a temporal, at least a spiritual entity. From Morocco in the west to
Java in the east, as far north as Samarkand and Granada, as far south as
Timbuktu, Islamic sovereigns ruled and Islamic traditions were
paramount. Even beyond, in east Africa, in the Himalayan frontier-
lands, in China itself, communities of Muslim traders formed thriving
enclaves, like stepping-stones across an infidel marsh. Compared with
Islam, Christianity was groping, Buddhism was impotent, Hinduism
was flaccid. Islam had survived the weakening of its former political
unity to remain one of the great power-factors of the world. The seven
great monarchs of the fourteenth-century world, in Ibn Batuta's
reckoning, were the Sultan of Morocco (naturally), the Sultan of

Egypt, the Sultan of the Two Iraqs, the Sultan of Turkistan, the Sultan of India, the Khan of the Golden Horde and the Emperor of China: six of the seven were Muslims.

For Islam was more than Empire, more even than a faith or an ideology. It was an entire manner of life, in which politics played a lesser part. Every aspect of human conduct was governed by its precepts. It was a religion, a style, a code of conduct, a loyalty, a system of law, a literature, a philosophy, a method of education, a language (for wherever Islam was honoured Arabic was understood). It was as though the Roman law, the Catholic faith and the social nuances of the British Empire were all to be combined in an all-embracing arrangement of society. The wandering Roman could cry *civis Romanus sum*, wherever he went in the world of the Caesars. The wandering Catholic could confess in Latin anywhere. The wandering Briton, if he knew the right people, could be sure of getting into a decent club from Halifax to Ootacamund. The wandering Muslim could expect more still, especially if he was a learned man of religion: everywhere, whatever the political condition of the country, co-religionists would help him, guide him, put him up, hear his case, introduce him, offer him letters of credit and see him safely on his way. It was like an immense freemasonry, expressed not only in human relationships and legal practice, but in the grand mosques of Islamic architecture, in the caravanserais of the pilgrim routes, in the common treasury of Arab legend and tradition, in the music of the Arabic tongue and the shared conviction that there was one God alone, and Mohammed was his prophet.

No wonder a Muslim was proud of his faith. Being Muslim was like winning, as Cecil Rhodes said of another condition, first prize in the lottery of life. The Empire of Islam might be disintegrating but the idea of Islam was as powerful as ever, and every Muslim felt himself inherently privileged. The Islamic potentates of the world bore themselves with immense splendour and confidence: Islamic soldiers, if relatively few of them now believed that death in a righteous battle would mean their instant translation to Paradise, certainly assumed Allah to be on their side—had they not, after all, triumphantly expelled the Christian Crusaders from the holy places of Palestine? The crescent of Islam was more than a holy talisman, but a sign of brotherhood too, and a reminder of common triumphs and aspirations.

So the world of Islam, hard though it was to define politically, really did constitute a civilization. Pre-eminent in philosophy, in astronomy, in mathematics, in poetry, in navigation, Islam held in trust for posterity the learning of the classical past. As a fructifying force the faith spread learning and speculation all over the medieval world, so that the peripatetic Muslim scholars of the age—Ibn Jubair, Ibn Khaldun, Ibn Batuta himself—were like agents of fertility, passing ideas from one continent to another. Muslims dominated the great trade routes of the earth: from the Mediterranean into Europe, into the Black Sea, into central Africa, through Persia to India and Malaya, through the East Indies to China. Islam was inescapable. Arabic words had entered the Icelandic language, Arabic numerals were used in England, Islamic law governed the affairs of Malacca as of Malaga. Throughout the east every large city had its Muslim quarter, its minaret, its local *qadi*. At sunset, in towns from Tangier to Amoy, hearts were turned towards Mecca and hopes towards Paradise.

*   *   *

It was into this rich, diverse, scattered and politically decadent society that the young Ibn Batuta had set off upon his travels just thirty years before. His first destination was the classic objective of Islam, Mecca itself, but before he laid down his staff at last in Abu Inan's capital of Fez, he was to have seen such sights as no Muslim had ever seen before, and many declined to believe in.

He travelled for three decades, sometimes staying put for years at a time, sometimes beginning a new journey almost the moment he finished the last. His itinerary was wayward. He made the pilgrimage to the Hejaz six times, and he went to India specifically to seek employment in the service of the powerful and ferocious Sultan Mohammed Tughlak. Otherwise he simply wandered, impulsively, when the spirit moved him, when somebody offered him safe conduct, when a junk unexpectedly sailed, when he discovered a fancy to see a strange country or interview some celebrated ascetic. Early in his travelling life he resolved that he would never follow the same route twice, and a map of his journeys looks like the route of some aimless or demented mendicant, all loops and backtracks, sudden forays and purposeless detours.

For thirty years his relatives and friends in Morocco could never be sure where he was, and along the way he picked up and discarded wives, as he bought and sold slaves, with an easy abandon: but fitfully news of him passed along the Islamic grapevine, so that he was heard of now in Turkestan, now in Ceylon, commanding a military campaign in India or investigating the flow of the Niger. In the further east they called him Shams-ed-Din, God's Sun; for he did seem to move in some inscrutable more or less diurnal motion, now shining in success, now dimmed in disfavour (at which times it was his custom, one cannot help observing, to spend more than his usual time at the mosque).

During those thirty years Ibn Batuta saw all the Maghreb, the north African coast, and all of what we would now call the Middle East, from Yemen and Aden in the south to Constantinople in the north. He visited the Arab settlements of east Africa, and passed through the northern borderlands of Turkey, where the emergent Ottomans were establishing themselves as brutal rulers, into the Crimea, the Caucasus and far into Kazakhstan. Passing through Afghanistan into India, he spent eight years in the service of the Sultan, before setting out on a disastrous official mission to China, in the course of which he lost all his possessions but acquired four wives and became *qadi* of the Maldive Islands—'I know', the Sultan had said, commissioning him for this embassy, 'your love of travel.' From China he returned via India and Arabia to Morocco, and after a visit to Moorish Spain spent the last two years of his travelling in the almost unknown kingdoms of west Africa. He retired to Fez at last in 1354, and spent the rest of his life remembering it all, dying in 1378 when he was seventy-three.

Such a bald narrative can give no idea of the scope, richness and variety of his travels. He was the traveller *par excellence*, the born wanderer, to whom new scenes, new faces, new experiences were the breath of life. Restless, volatile, emotional, rather greedy, not very profound, distinctly pleased with himself, he nevertheless possessed all the attributes of the good traveller. He was endlessly curious. He was not easily offended. He never pretended to be anything but what he was, a gentleman and scholar of the Maghreb. He relished the pleasures of travel, and forgot the miseries unless they were interesting. He was adept at generalization, an essential aspect of the travelling art. Trained to egalitarianism by Islam, a faith of equals, while he had a keen eye for the main chance and the princely munificence, still he preferred plain speaking and no kow-tow. He was generous. He was tough. Above all he possessed the gift of serendipity, and stumbled through life from one astonishment to another, whether it was the mythical bird called the roc, which ate elephants and which he thought he saw in the Indian Ocean, or the giant cocks of Cathay, which were as big as ostriches, and were sometimes featherless, or the tree in Ceylon whose leaves never withered, but around whose trunk a community of holy men had settled, waiting year in year out, autumn after autumn, for the day of the fall.

Sometimes he was rich and influential, sometimes he was destitute, sometimes he was only a wandering scholar, sometimes a political grandee, possessing so many horses, as he once remarked, that he dare not mention the number 'in case some sceptic should call me a liar'. Here we see him as chief justice of the Maldives, ruthlessly reforming the morals of the islanders but plotting to overthrow the regime with the help of the King of Coromandel. Here, on the beach at Calicut, he abjectly watches a renegade junk sail away with all his possessions, leaving him only with one enfranchised slave boy—'and when he saw what had happened he deserted me, and I had nothing left at all except ten dinars and the carpet I had slept on.' Here he is welcomed with honour to the tents of the Khan of the Golden Horde, a vast mobile city with its own mosques and bazaars, its ceremonial Golden Pavilion, its thousands of horses and wagons and the smoke perpetually rising from its hundreds of kitchens. Here, on the other hand, stripped of sandals, turban and sash, he sits on the ground somewhere south of Delhi waiting to be hanged by the brigands who have captured him, and have placed at his feet the hempen rope of execution. When, with his entourage of forty persons, he arrived at Delhi the Sultan gave him a hospitality gift of a furnished house, 6,000 silver dinars, large quantities of meat, sugar, ghee, nuts and betel-leaves, and the annual revenue of several villages. When he arrived at Malli, in west Africa, with an entourage of five, the Sultan gave him a welcome gift of three cakes, a piece of fried beef and a calabash of sour curds.

This at least is how he tells it all. Nobody ever described Ibn Batuta himself, and only two contemporary works have references to him, neither very flattering—his stories were often, like Marco Polo's, greeted with reserve. Some people perhaps distrusted his memory, which must have indeed been remarkable. Others took him for a plain liar, and flatly disbelieved his tales about the monkey-chiefs of Ceylon, who lean on staves of office and are attended by monkey-courtiers, or his eyewitness accounts of the Indian rope trick, or his rats bigger than cats, or his houses made of fish-bones in the Kuria Muria Islands. Modern scholars have confirmed that most of what he said is accurate: and though there are certainly chronological blurs in his narrative, and some hazy topographic moments too, especially when he approaches the Rampart of Gog and Magog in northern China, still for myself I prefer to accept it all as gospel truth, if not as history, at least as art.

I believe him implicitly, for example, when he tells us that locusts cannot fly when they are cold, or that African cannibals believe white people to be unripe. I accept absolutely his claim that the males of Barahnakar, though otherwise shaped like humans, have snouts like dogs. And, in particular, I find his dialogue wonderfully authentic. In the 'country of Tawalisi', a place otherwise unknown to geography, he met a princess of warlike tastes, who commanded a corps of Amazons and often engaged in single combat herself. This fierce lady, who was Governor of Kaylukari, was much taken by Ibn Batuta's descriptions of India, and decided she would like to conquer that country. 'I must', she drawled, 'positively make an expedition to it, and take possession of it myself, for the quantity of its riches and its troops attracts me.'

Ibn Batuta had been on the road for twenty years, and knew all about women. 'Do so,' he simply replied, and left it at that.

* * *

If it is not always true in the detail, it is certainly true in the sweep, and Ibn Batuta's memoirs form an incomparable panorama of eastern life in the fourteenth century. The story is built around the great trade and pilgrim routes of the Islamic world, with their long-established habits of loyalty, comradeship and peculation: Islam was so institutionalized, so set in its ways of morality and tradition, that around its highways a society of the roads had long been established, ranging from the thieves who beset the pilgrim routes to the Young Brotherhood who courteously ushered the traveller from town to town in Syria, or the sheikhs and *qadis* who welcomed distinguished visitors to their communities. Ibn Batuta's passage through this fraternity, often with introductions, always with the credentials of his faith and learning, gives to his narrative some kind of theme, just as its existence gave a tenuous cohesion to the shambled Muslim world. He suggests to me sometimes some modern Christian evangelical, welcomed with coffee and crackers in manse or rectory along his holiday route: but if this routine of travel had to it elements of the humdrum, even of the touristic, it was relieved constantly by magnificent interludes of danger, pageantry or exotica.

There was the terrific moment, for example, when his patroness, a daughter of the Byzantine Emperor Andronicus III, having fled from her marriage to the Tartar chieftain Mohammed Uzbeg, was met outside Constantinople by her brother Prince Qaras. What a sight that was! From the east rode the prince, attended by 5,000 horsemen. Five more princes rode at his right hand, five at his left, and they were dressed all in white, with gold-embroidered parasols above their heads, and preceded by lancers in chain-mail, and surrounded by fluttering standards, and heralded by drums, bugles, trumpets and fifes. From the west rode the princess, home from the Tartars, surrounded by maidens, slaves, eunuchs and Mongol guards, all dressed in silk. She was in gold brocade, and on her head she wore a crown, and her horse was embellished everywhere with gold. On a flat green space these gorgeous cortèges met: Prince Qaras, dismounting, kissed his sister's foot; Princess Bayalun kissed her brother's head; and so the two companies joined, and turning towards the Bosporus in a glitter of jewels, a discord of trumpets and a shimmer of golden fabrics, proceeded to Constantinople.

Or take, in quite another kind, the spectacle at the top of Adam's Peak in Ceylon, which Ibn Batuta reported to be one of the tallest mountains in the world (it is 7,400 feet high). This was a place of pilgrimage for Muslims, Buddhists and Hindus alike because of the holy footprint upon its summit—Adam's to the Muslims, Buddha's to the Buddhists, Shiva's to the Hindus. Holy men and mendicants of every kind made the journey there, pulling themselves up the mountain with iron chains until, on a black rock near the summit, they saw the blessed footprint. For Ibn Batuta this was one of the great moments of travel. He had seen the mountain from the sea nine days before, and by the time he approached the summit the land below was magically veiled in cloud, and the holy destination was isolated in the sky. His most vivid description of the experience, though, concerned a less than spiritual impulse. In the hollow of the footprint pilgrims used to place votive offerings of gold or jewellery. When the wilder supplicants approached the summit of the mountain, Ibn Batuta recalls, they raced each other up the last steep stretch not to kiss the holy ground, but to get the votive offerings; and how clearly we see them still through the lines of his narrative, ragged dervishes from Sind, Sumatra or Afghanistan, their tattered clothes streaming, their faces grimaced, as they scrambled up the rock face, pushing and jostling each other, to fall gasping upon the sacred relic and grab its gold!

Ibn Batuta had a fine eye for the quirk or the incongruity. In the Land of Darkness, he tells us (by which he means, as Marco Polo did,

Siberia), traders from the outside world simply left their wares in an empty clearing in the forest, returning to their tents for the night: when they returned in the morning they would find that the indigenes had substituted their own furs and hides, thus completing the transaction without ever showing themselves to strangers—perhaps they were not humans at all, Ibn Batuta mildly surmises, but jinn. In Qaqula, he tells us (which may have been in Java, and may have been in Malaya) every house had its own elephant picketed at the door, and the shopkeepers kept elephants at the store, too, to deliver the groceries and ride home in the evening. In India he saw a widow, raising her hands sacramentally to the fire, throw herself into the funeral pyre of suttee. In the Maldives he stayed with a weaver who lived alone on a small island with his family, a boat and a few coconut palms—'and I swear I envied that man, and wished that the island had been mine, and that I might have made it my retreat until the inevitable hour should befall me.'

He loved the marvellous and the mythical, and was perhaps too ready to believe in the miracles of Muslim saints, or the virtuosities of magicians. But he did his best to be objective. Once he was introduced to a holy man said to be 350 years old, who looked about fifty and said he grew new teeth and hair every hundred years—'but', said Ibn Batuta reluctantly, 'I had some doubts about him . . .' He was even non-committal about the roc, one of the supreme fables of medieval times: the sailors on his ship had no doubts at all, when they saw a vast black shadow above the horizon, but Ibn Batuta himself thought it looked like an island—and it probably was, distorted by refraction. In China a well-known wizard, having sent his boy assistant into the air on an unsuspended rope, climbed up after him and threw his dismembered body to the floor below, later putting all its limbs together again and restoring it to life. Ibn Batuta needed potions to restore him from the shock of this demonstration, but he quotes with approval, at least in retrospect, the opinion of one of his companions: 'By God, there was no climbing or coming down or cutting up of limbs at all—the whole thing is just hocus-pocus!'

* * *

Like all the best travellers, Ibn Batuta had strong views about the places he visited and the people he met. Infidels, of course, were *a priori* inferiors, and even the grandest heathen, a king or minister of state, he would sometimes greet with the backhanded courtesy:

'Peace be upon those who follow the true religion.' He found some races, in any case, distinctly more congenial than others. Nowhere in the world, for instance, were there more excellent people than the Khwarizmians of the Uzbeg country, who were generous, hospitable, and whipped all absentees from morning prayer: on the other hand nobody could be much worse than the Russians, who were red-haired and blue-eyed, had ugly treacherous faces and were Christian. The Maldivians were upright, pious, sound in belief and sincere in thought: the people of Iwalatan, in the Sahara, were ill mannered, racially arrogant and promiscuous. The most gifted people in the world were the Chinese, the most submissive, but the most resolute against injustice, were the Negroes.

Yet though he excelled in these sweeping judgements, and relished everything that was spacious and opulent, still it is the details of daily life that give his work its conviction and its style. One remembers best not the panorama, but the glimpse. Here the Uzbeg prince Qutludumur, reclining on a silk carpet with his feet covered because of the gout, serves a repast of roasted fowls, cranes and pomegranates, some offered in gold vessels with golden spoons, but others (for eating out of gold was anathema to the strictest Muslims) in glass vessels with wooden spoons. Here the benevolent Sharif Jalal ad-Din al-Kiji of Uja, being about to leave on a protracted journey, casually offers Ibn Batuta a farewell gift: 'Take my village,' he says. We catch sight of the mighty black Abyssinians who, marshalled between the decks of junks, kept the pirates of the Indian Ocean at bay; we meet a slave-governor of India who eats a whole sheep at a meal; we observe our traveller, muffled against the cold of Astrakhan in three fur coats, two pairs of trousers and three pairs of boots, shaking the frozen water from his beard when he washes, and unable to mount his horse without a push from behind. Here is Ibn Batuta in the middle of the Uzbeg desert, half-way between Khiva and Bokhara, in a country seldom visited by westerners before, and rich in mystery and allure. What does he remember best, and recall most tellingly? Not the desolation of it all, not the remoteness, the cold or the danger, but the small boys playing and sliding on the ice of a frozen lake near Kat.

It was an exhausting life, and sometimes Ibn Batuta momentarily lost heart, withdrawing to the mosque to lick his wounds, or even, in India, 'disentangling himself from the world' as the disciple of a troglodytic fakir. Now and then he offers a tart response, when his patience is wearing thin, or finds it politic to move on, when he has rubbed a sultan up the wrong way. He seldom grumbles, though, for there is nothing like travel to broaden one's philosophy. In Turkey he employed an Arabic-speaking fellow pilgrim to do the shopping for him, only to discover that the rascal habitually fiddled the expenses, pocketing the surplus for himself. A lesser traveller would have lost his temper, but Ibn Batuta knew better. He knew the value of compromise, and confined himself to a wry evening quip, at the end of each day's journey: 'Well, Hajji, how much have you stolen today?'

*   *   *

When Ibn Batuta retired at last to Morocco, the world he had wandered had recognizably crumbled since his first pilgrimage thirty years before. The Byzantine Empire was in its last decades. The Ottomans were nearly ready to fall upon Constantinople. The Sultanate of Delhi was disintegrating. The Sultanate of Egypt was so racked by inner rivalries that between 1341 and 1351 eight different mamelukes briefly occupied the throne. In Spain the Muslim provinces were being whittled away one by one, in Europe the Christians were stirring again in the first portentous enterprises of the Renaissance. Anarchy threatened half Islam. Yet still the Islamic civilization survived, and even today one may recognize its flavour and its spirit, and experience many of the sensations of travel that Ibn Batuta recorded six centuries ago.

The art and architecture of Islam, for example, still set the tone of great cities through the east—some still ruled by Muslim governments, some by infidels. The magnificent mosques that Ibn Batuta visited— the Kaaba at Mecca, the Dome of the Rock at Jerusalem, the Great Mosque at Damascus—all remain to this day places of sanctity and retreat, where one may still meet those learned holy men who were Ibn Batuta's hosts and confrères, where the carpets still lie in the shade of the prayer-hall, where the students sit cross-legged at their books, where the muezzin still sings his call to prayer at sunrise, even if he is electrically amplified through the loudspeakers dangling insouciantly from those glorious minarets. The Muslim travel routes of Ibn Batuta's day are still recognizable. The broad track of the Hejaz pilgrimage, worn by the feet of a million camels through 700 years of dedication, still stretches away into the deserts of Arabia. The caravans still lurch their passage through the Khyber, Islam's traditional entry into India. The dhows still cross from Aden to trade with the Muslims on the African coast. The road from Morocco to Mali still passes, as Ibn

Batuta did, by way of Timbuktu. The immemorial chains still hang to help the pilgrims up the dizzy precipices of Adam's Peak.

Metaphysically, too, many of Ibn Batuta's impressions apply today. His ritual panegyric still wonderfully captures the amplitude of Cairo, familiar still to infatuates of that incomparable city: 'Mother of cities and seat of Pharaoh the tyrant, mistress of broad regions and fruitful lands, boundless in multitude of buildings, peerless in beauty and splendour, the meeting-place of comer and goer, the halting-place of feeble and mighty, whose throngs surge as the waves of the sea, and can scarce be contained in her for all her size and capacity.' The golden fragrance of Shiraz and Isfahan, the dour splendour of Constantinople, the green relief of the Damascene orchards—across the gulf of so many years Ibn Batuta offers us their true essence even now, and so becomes our own contemporary.

More clearly still, all too clearly sometimes, can we recognize in his narrative the ironies or nuisances of travel, and the characters who haunt the traveller's path as unavoidably now as they did then. Who has not met Ibn Batuta's fulsome Turkish judge, who asked so flatteringly about all his experiences, who said he simply *must* come home for dinner one day, and who is never heard from again? Who has not met the pious Sheikh Abdullah of Bursa, who seemed to have been *everywhere* that Ibn Batuta chanced to mention? (Ah, but he never got to China!) Who does not remember the well-known local linguist who, confronted at last by an importunate arrival, resorts to the dim excuse that he speaks a different *kind* of Arabic/Welsh/Hindi/Chinese? We have all suffered from the indispensable guide who loses the way, the sailors who say the tide's too high, the kind host whose hospitality sours by Monday morning, the Cassandras, the provincial know-alls, the officious functionaries and the inescapable busybodies who infested Ibn Batuta's passage so long ago.

The bureaucracy of travel was hardly less ubiquitous then, for endemic to the Islamic system was a love of regulation. At Constantinople Ibn Batuta was frisked, before entering the Emperor's throne-room, as routinely as he would be at the airport now. At the Indian frontier he discovered that intelligence reports about him had already been forwarded to Delhi, and a local judge, with notaries, had to witness his application for a visa. It was odd how often reports about him reached foreign countries before he got there himself, and noticeable how often emissaries from local despots greeted and questioned him the moment he arrived in town. Ibn Batuta would be quite at home in today's suspicious world: and just as the modern western innocent, reaching his first dictatorship, is appalled by the evidence of autocracy all around, so Ibn Batuta, visiting his first Christian city, Feodosia on the Black Sea, is appalled by the clamour of the church bells, a sound forbidden to Muslims, and as weird as it was wicked to a holy man from the Maghreb.

*   *   *

Yet if much is familiar, more is gone. Ibn Batuta tells us that when he went back to Alexandria in 1349, after twenty years' absence, he found the great Pharos lighthouse, bequeathed to the Muslims by an earlier culture, in a melancholy state of decay: a structure which had been nearly complete in his first visit was now hardly more than a ruin. Today whole cities of his own civilization have vanished from the map, ports that were crammed with junks and dhows are no more than silted creeks, great capitals have lost their consequence, nations and tribes are forgotten or even exterminated. The Byzantines provide an eponym of decadence; the Golden Horde is no more than a romantic legend; even the rampaging Ottomans presently became the Sick Men of Europe, before vanishing from the stage.

Ibn Batuta could hardly escape the early signs of this decline. He was not, though, a didactic traveller, not one to draw conclusions. He wandered as a way of life, and he drew no particular lessons from his journeying, except perhaps gratitude to God—'who hath subdued the earth to His servants that they may tread thereon'. His purposes were instinctive, and probably addictive too. He was an opportunist, like all good travellers, and he was a fatalist, like all good Muslims, living for the day and its own revelations. Still, if he learnt no lessons from his journeys, we can learn some from his example: not only technical tips—how many towels you are entitled to in the Baghdad public baths (three), or what to expect at a Tartar royal funeral (the burial of live slaves)—but historical lessons too.

The first interest of Ibn Batuta's memoirs lies in their immediacy, which make us see those antique spectacles as though for ourselves. The deeper fascination, though, lies in their context. The setting was that of a once paramount civilization fast relapsing into fissiparous units, and held together only by a cultural heritage. Within that setting, nevertheless, our traveller moves still along familiar paths, insulated by manners of thought and conviction against the political convulsions occurring all around.

Since then more than one great culture has come and gone, and today we see around us, perhaps, the decay of that particular structure of ethics and method which evolved from the European Renaissance— the successor, in fact, to the Empire of the Muslims. We too live in a world where political certainties are shakier than they were, where one can no longer depend upon the Stars and Stripes or the Union Jack to give us security, where infidels of every category are succeeding to power.

Yet the good traveller, even now, need not find himself alienated. Everywhere he can discover, as Ibn Batuta did, oases and enclaves of his own culture, still surviving the fall of dynasties or the eclipse of ideologies, still ready to welcome him and give him, if not an elephant or a pomegranate in a golden bowl, at least a novel to read or an invitation to share the Thanksgiving turkey. Civilization is not *only* in the beholder's eye: it is in the eye of time, too, and what was barbarism to one generation becomes finesse to the next. Nothing is permanent in the world. Nothing is indispensable. Standards, like kingdoms, come and go.

Only the Traveller, impervious to change, journeys always on.

'DO YOU THINK SHOULD HE HAVE GONE OVER?'

When I went to Dublin once, I found that the very next morning the fifth President of the Irish Republic, the *Uachtarán*, was to be installed in the Hall of St. Patrick in Dublin Castle. Hastening out to buy myself a proper dress ('I congratulate you,' said the maid at my hotel in some surprise, 'you've got excellent taste'), and procuring an official pass (*Preas, Insealbhu an Uchtardín*), promptly in the morning I presented myself at the Castle gates, made my way through the confusion of soldiery, officialdom and diplomacy that filled the old yard, and found my place beside the dais in the elegantly decorated hall ('No place for purple prose,' murmured my cicerone pointedly, 'more the Ionian white and gold.')

It was a delightful occasion. All Eire was there, among the massed banners and crests of the ancient Irish provinces, beneath the stern gaze of the trumpeters poised for their fanfare in the minstrels' gallery. All the Ministers were there, with their invisible portfolios. All the Ambassadors were there, with their distinctly visible wives. *Both* Primates of All Ireland were there, side by side in parity. There were judges and surgeons, old revolutionaries and new politicians, clerics by the hundred, professors by the score. There was Conor Cruise O'Brien. There was John Lynch. There was Sean MacBride the Nobel Laureate. There was Cyril Cusack the actor. It was like seeing the Irish Republic encapsulated, dressed in its newest fineries, sworn to its best behaviour, and deposited in the building which, more than any other in Ireland, speaks of Irish history.

The new President, Cearbhall O Dalaigh, seemed a dear man indeed, and gave us a gentle rambling speech much concerned with what the removal men said when they packed his possessions for the move. Some of it was in Gaelic, some in French, some in English, and I confess my mind did wander now and then, towards the Ruritanian

Ambassadress's fur coat, towards the twin smiles of the Archbishops, towards the fierce survey of the bandmaster high above, who might easily have stepped from the ranks of the old Connaught Rangers. One phrase in particular, though, and not alas the President's own, caught my attention. It was a quotation from Thoreau, and it ran thus: 'If a man does not keep pace with his companions, perhaps it is because he hears a different drummer.'

A different drummer! What drummer beat in Dublin now, I wondered, where the best were always out of step? What pace would the bandmaster set today? Was the drum-beat different still, in this most defiantly different of capitals?

*   *   *

That evening, when the dignitaries, officials and soldiers had dispersed to their celebratory banquets (all except the poor military policeman who, vainly trying to kick his motor-bike to life, was left forlorn in the Castle yard to a universal sigh of sympathy), I drove along the coast to Howth, and then the Joyceness of Dublin, the Yeatsness, the pubness, the tramness, the Liffeyness, the Behanness, in short the stock Dublinness of the place seemed to hang like a vapour over the distant city. It was one of those Irish evenings when the points of the compass seem to have been confused, and their climates with them. A bitter east wind swayed the palm trees along the promenade, a quick northern air sharpened that slightly Oriental languor, that Celtic *dolce far niente*, which habitually blurs the intentions of Dublin. Over the water the city lay brownish below the Wicklow Mountains, encrusted it seemed with some tangible patina of legend and literature, and fragrant of course with its own *vin du pays*, Guinness.

This is everyone's Dublin, right or wrong, and if it is partly myth, it is substance too. There is no such thing as a stage Dubliner: the characters of this city, even at their most theatrical, are true and earnest in their kind, and Dublin too, even today, lives up to itself without pretence. Are there any urchins like Dublin urchins, grubby as sin and bouncy as ping-pong balls? Are there any markets like Dublin markets, sprawling all over the city streets like gipsy jumble sales? Are there any buses so evocative as Dublin buses, lurching in dim-lit parade towards Glasnevin?

Certainly there are few more boisterous streets on earth than O'Connell Street on a Saturday night, when a salt wind gusts up from the sea, making the girls giggle and the young men clown about, driving the Dublin litter helter-skelter here and there, and eddying the smells of beer, chips and hot-dogs all among the back streets. And there is no café more tumultuous than Bewley's Oriental Café in Grafton Street, with its mountains of buns on every table, with its children draped over floors and chairs, with its harassed waitresses scribbling, its tea-urns hissing, its stained glass and its tiled floors, its old clock beside the door, the high babel of its Dublin chatter and its haughty Dublin ladies, all hats and arched eyebrows, smoking their cigarettes loftily through it all.

It is an all too familiar rhythm, but it beats unmistakably still, hilariously and pathetically, and it makes of Dublin one of the most truly exotic cities in the world. One still finds shawled beggar women on the Liffey bridges at night, huddling their babies close, attended by wide-eyed small boys and holding cardboard boxes for contributions. One still hears the instant give-and-take in Dublin pubs and parlours. 'Ah, me rheumatism's cured,' says the old lady quick as a flash when the landlord pats her kindly on the knee, 'you should advertise your healing powers.' 'Sure it was only my left hand too,' says the landlord. 'Well and it was only my left knee—try the other one there's a good man.' I experienced the tail-end of a bank robbery in Dublin one day, and only in this city, I thought, could I observe the principal witness of a crime interviewed by the police in a butcher's shop—between whose ranks of hanging turkeys, from the pavement outside, I could glimpse his blood-streaked face enthusiastically recalling the horror of it all.

Dublin's gay but shabby recklessness, too, which so infuriated its English overlords, brazenly survives. If there is a public clock that works in Dublin, I have yet to find it, and I was not in the least surprised when, calling at a restaurant at a quarter to five to arrange a table for dinner, I found several jolly parties concluding their lunch. The Irish honour their own priorities still. 'It's not very satisfactory just to tell your customers', I overheard a lady complaining at the G.P.O., 'that the mail's gone up with a bomb, it's not very satisfactory at all.' 'He'll make a fine President,' somebody said to me of Cearbhall O Dalaigh, 'nobody knows what his name is.' 'Enjoy yourself now!' everybody says in Dublin, and they mean enjoy yourself *notwithstanding*.

Dublin is very old—old in history, old in style. If there is no such thing as a stage Dubliner, in a curious way there is no such thing as a young one, either. The dry scepticism of the Dublin manner, the elliptical nature of its conversations, the dingy air of everything, the retrospection—all conspire to give this city a sense of elderly collusion.

Everyone seems to know everyone else, and all about him too. Go
into any Dublin company, somebody suggested to me one day, and
present the cryptic inquiry: 'Do you think should he have gone over?'
Instantly, whatever the circumstances, there will be a cacophony of
replies. 'Sure he should, but not without telling his wife'—'And why
shouldn't he have, was he not the elected representative?'—'Well it
wasn't so far as it looked'—'It didn't surprise me, his father was just
the same.' Such is the accumulated familiarity of the city that to any
inquiry, about anybody, about anything, every Dubliner—every true
Dubberlin man, as the vernacular has it—possesses an infallible response,
usually wrong.

Such a sense of commonalty curdles easily into conspiracy, and of
course history has helped to fuse your Dubliners, making them feel
far more homogeneous than the people of most western capitals. This
is not only a classless society, at least in externals, it is an indigenous one
too. Your Italian waiter, your Chinese take-away *restaurateur*, your
Jamaican bus conductor, even your Nigerian student of computer
technology are all rare figures in Dublin still, and the consequent
unity of method and temper gives the city much of its exuberant punch.

It also gives it a special pride, for this is not only the capital of a
nation, but the capital of an idea. The idea of Irishness is not universally
beloved. Some people mock it, some hate it, some fear it. On the
whole, though, I think it fair to say, the world interprets it chiefly as
a particular kind of happiness, a happiness sometimes boozy and
violent, but essentially innocent: and this ineradicable spirit of merri-
ment informs the Dublin genius to this day, and is alive and bubbling
still, for all the miseries of the Irish Problem, in this jumbled brown
capital across the water.

*   *   *

Sometimes I could hear other drummers, though. I rang up the
Dáil one day and asked if there was anything interesting to observe
that evening. 'There's always me,' said the usher, 'I'm interesting.'
For if on one level Dublin is a world capital, to which subjects from
Melbourne to the Bronx pay a vicarious or morganatic allegiance,
on another it is the day-to-day capital of a little state. In this it is very
modern. Ireland seems to me the right size for a country, the truly
contemporary size, the size at which regionalism properly becomes
nationhood, and the parliamentary usher answers the telephone
himself. Small units within a large framework offer a sensible pattern

for the world's future, and beneath the fustiness of the old Dublin, the world's Dublin, a much more contemporary entity exists.

Old Dublin is averse to change, but this smaller, inner Dublin welcomes it. 'If I know the Brits,' said a genial enthusiast at a Balls-bridge party, holding my hand and talking about London, 'they'll soon be having St. Paul's down to make way for a new ghastly office block.' Well, the Micks are not much better when it comes to urban development. Visual taste is hardly their forte, and they have done little to improve the look of Dublin since the end of the Ascendancy. Wide areas of the Liberties are in that melancholy state of unexplained decay that generally precedes 'improvement', there are frightful plans for the Liffey quays, the Central Bank is building itself a structure which is not only grossly out of scale with the time and the city, but seems in its present state of completion to be made of Meccano—'an awful thing in itself', as a bystander observed to me, 'and terrible by implication'.

More often the implications of change are merely sad. They imply a deliberate, functional rejection not perhaps of tradition or principle, but of habit. Gone is many an ancient pub, anomalous perhaps to a condition of progress, but beloved in itself. Crippled is many a Georgian square. Doomed and derelict is J. J. Byrne the fish shop ('This Is The Place'). Fearful ring roads threaten. No good looking in for Dublin Bay prawns at the old Red Bank: it was long ago converted into a Catholic chapel, where in the Dublin manner the local girls slip in for a moment's supplication before rejoining their boy friends on the pavement outside for a stout in the corner bar.

There are worse things to worry about, too. There are the Troubles, those endemic mysteries of Ireland, which are inescapable in Dublin if only by suggestion—*Beál Feirste*, as the road signs say, is only 100 miles to the north. A fairly muzzy security screen protects the offices of the Irish Government, and sends the unsuspecting visitor backwards and forwards between the guards—'Did you not see this young lady when she came in?' 'I did not, she must have walked by like a ghost.' When I saw a big black car with two big men in it, standing outside my host's suburban house, I knew a Minister was calling, and I looked more than once over my shoulder before, in a spirit of pure inquiry, I entered the house in Parnell Square where they sell Christmas cards and *objets d'art* made by the internees of Ulster.

But far more immediate than the bomber is the rising price. In Britain inflation is merely another blow to the punch-drunk: in

Ireland it is an unfair decision. For so many centuries a loser, in recent years Eire has found a winning streak, finding its feet at last, establishing its place in the world, evolving a mean between the practical and the ideal, forgiving and even half-forgetting the tragedies of the past. With change, it seemed, prosperity was coming. Many of the new buildings of Dublin might be unlovely, but at least they were earnests of success.

Now the poor Dubliners find themselves haunted once again by the prospect of failure. The Irish economy is less than hefty, and could not long resist a world recession. Then the brief holiday would be over, the cars would be sold, the colour televisions sold, the plump young Dublin executive would no longer be lunching at a quarter to five. You might not guess the possibility from the Grafton Street stores, which are among the most charming and fastidious in Europe, but your Dubberlin man sees it plain enough, and often speaks of it with cheerful foreboding, as he chooses a third sticky cake at Bewley's, or summons a second bottle of hock.

For luckily Dublin's rueful optimism survives, and pervades the Republic too. They said some fairly gloomy things in the *Dáil* that evening, and discussed some daunting prospects, but when they adjourned for a vote, and the deputies hung over the rail of the Chamber waiting for the tellers, with their rubicund laughing faces, their stocky country frames, their irrepressible chatter and their elbows on the rail, I thought they looked for all the world like convivial farmers at a cattle sale, looking down towards the Speaker's chair as towards the auctioneer, and waiting for the next Friesian to be led in from the robing chamber. 'Didja enjoy yourself now?' said the usher when I left, and the security man in his little lodge waggled his fingers at me as I passed.

I suppose there are terrorists plotting in Dublin, and bombers preparing their fuses, but it remains, all the same, pre-eminently the innocent capital of a star-crossed state—for the luck of the Irish is a wish more than a characteristic. One of its greatest charms is its intimate completeness. There are only 3 million people in Eire, scarcely more than there are in Wales, but Dublin has its diplomatic corps and its Government departments, its *Uachtarán*, its *Taoiseach* and all the trappings of a sovereign capital. Irish pictures, Irish plays, Irish artefacts, Irish heroes—Dublin is obsessed with itself and its hinterland, giving the little capital a character introspective perhaps but undeniably authoritative, for it is certainly the last word on itself.

Half its pleasure lies in its pride. Ten columns of the Dublin telephone book are needed to list the 660 institutions which boast the prefix 'Irish'. Like the Welsh and Scots, but unlike the hapless English, the Irish are still frankly affectionate towards their nationality, and this gives Dubliners an unexpected balance or serenity. I went one night to the Abbey Theatre, where Mr. Cusack was playing the Vicar of Wakefield as to the manner born, and thought as I looked at the audience around me how enviably *natural* they looked. The burden of their history did not show, and they were not entangled by inhibitions of power or prestige. They had never been citizens of a Great Power, and never would be. They talked in no phoney accents, pined for no lost empires, and laughed at Goldsmith's gentle humour without much caring whether the world laughed too.

For if Dublin is parochial, it is not provincial exactly, for it remains original. British influences are ubiquitous, it is true, from the Aldershot drill of the Presidential guard to *Coronation Street* on Monday evening, but there is no sense of copy-cat. Dubliners are their own men still. Even when a concern is foreign owned, as so many in Dublin are, it acquires a distinctively Irish flavour, so that even Trust House-Fortes' Airport Hotel coffee-shop, physically a carbon of every airport coffee-shop ever built anywhere, will give you eggs and bacon at lunch time if you ask nicely, 'for sure the chef's a kindly man'.

And though it is small, still Dublin feels like a true capital. Like Edinburgh, it deserves sovereignty. It is a fine thing to walk through the Dublin streets on a Sunday morning, say, when the sun is rising brilliantly out of the Bay, and to see the monuments of Irish pride around you—the fire on Parnell's column, O'Connell the Liberator on his plinth, the great columns of the Customs House, the delicate dome of the Four Courts. Over the great bridge you go, where the wind off the Bay sweeps up-river to blow your hair about, and there is Trinity before you, where Congreve and Swift and Burke were educated, where Goldsmith stands on his pedestal and the *Book of Kells* lies for ever open in its case. On your right is the old Irish Parliament, on the left is the City Hall, and soon, turning the cobbled corner at the top, you are—

Soon you are where? Why, back in the yard of Dublin Castle, where Presidents of Eire are installed indeed, but where for 800 years, in a presence far more monstrous, far more stately, the power of the English inexorably resided.

* * *

For like it or not, whatever your opinions, the drums of tragedy sound still in Dublin, muffled but unavoidable, as they sound nowhere else on earth. For eight centuries the Irish struggled against the dominion of the English, and it takes more than fifty uneasy years to silence the echoes.

The most compelling of all the figures at that Presidential occasion was that of Eamon de Valera, who arrived in an aged Rolls, and whose stiff blind figure, depending upon the arm of a veteran officer, leaning slightly backward as the blind sometimes do, and tapping with his stick between the silent lines of the diplomatic corps, cast a somewhat macabre hush upon the assembly. 'The skeleton at the feast,' whispered an irreverent observer somewhere near me, but I found the spectacle very moving; and when with difficulty the old rebel climbed the dais and sat ramrod-stiff on his chair a few feet away from me, holding his stick between his knees and sometimes decorously applauding, I envisaged all he had seen in the progress of the little state, the Easter Rising, the war against the British, the horrible Civil War, and so by way of plot and revolution, obstinacy and courage, deviousness and boldness, to the installation of the fifth *Uachtarán* there on the bright blue carpets of St. Patrick's Hall.

When I first knew Dublin, in the early 1960s, I thought the old fervours of revolution were fading, and that the memories of that sad struggle would die with its own generation. But the drum beats still, a drum to the treble of the Ulster fifes, and the presence there of Mr. de Valera did not seem an anachronism to me, only a grave reminder. The terrible beauty lingers still, tainted perhaps but inescapable. That evening, after dinner, I wandered alone among the back streets behind the General Post Office, where little more than fifty years ago the fated visionaries of the Rising fought and died among the blazing ruins.

It is smart in Dublin to denigrate the Easter Rising now, and to say that it achieved nothing after all, but still those streets seemed haunted ground to me. The glow of the burning Post Office lit the night sky still, the Soldier's Song sounded above the traffic, and at the end of every street I could see the barricades of the British, and hear the clatter of their rifles and the clink of their tea-mugs. Sometimes machine-guns rattled, and the awful smell of war, of death and dirt and cordite, hung all about the buildings. I wept as I remembered that old tragedy, and thought of those brave men so soon to be shot at dawn, and of the ignorant homely English at their guns behind their sandbags, and I turned towards home in a sad despair, contemplating the deceits of glory.

But when I turned into O'Connell Street I looked up into the plane trees, swaying above me in the night wind, and dimly I discerned there the grey shapes of the pied wagtails, those miraculous familiars of Dublin. Every winter those loyal country birds come back to roost in the trees of O'Connell Street, settling down each day at dusk, fluttering away to mountain and moorland when the dawn breaks. They calmed and comforted me at once, and I saw in their silent presence a figure of my own gratitude—for the gaiety that takes me back to Dublin year after year, for the melody that sounds always above the drums and bombs of Ireland, and for the old comradeship of this city, which transcends all bitterness, ignores time, and is the truest of Dublin's contradictory truths.

THROUGH MY GUIDE-BOOKS

When things get too awful, when the rain never seems likely to stop, and the toolmakers are striking, and Sam the dog has been rolling in manure—when life seems irredeemable, then I retreat to the lost world of my old guide-books. In that musty row of greens and browns all anxieties are sublimated, and nothing seems too dreadful. Fleas in Russia are only 'insects of a vexatory disposition'. Fish dishes in

Egypt merely have 'a strong flavour of mud'. Danish white port wine is no more than 'a remarkable combination'. Dr. Vaume, the French physician of Crete, may be alarming in the flesh, but in Murray's *Handbook to Greece* (1884), he simply has 'the reputation of using violent remedies'. Camels will meet trains on request at Jungshahi, prices of walking dresses in the rue de la Paix may generally be reduced by a little bargaining and the third-class travelling community in the Rhenish Provinces, so Herr Baedeker assures us, is generally quiet and respectable.

* * *

The heyday of the guide-book was the nineteenth century, when steam had made travel relatively easy, but the average tourist was still an educated person, able to appreciate Murray's donnish quirks or Baedeker's obscurer allusions to the principles of Gothic fenestration. There are felicities, of course, to be found both in earlier and in later examples. My favourite guide-book chapter, on the whole, is Chapter XII of Horrebow's *Iceland* (1758), which is entitled 'Concerning Owls in Iceland', and which consists in its entirety of one phrase: 'There are no owls of any kind in the whole island.' The guide-book advice I most admire is given by E. M. Forster in his *Alexandria* (1922)—'The best way to see it is to wander aimlessly about'—while one could hardly improve the opening to Chapter IV of Mrs. R. L. Devonshire's *Rambles in Cairo* (1931): 'Of all the medieval rulers of Egypt, Saladin alone enjoys the privilege of being remembered by Western readers.' In our own time Mr. David Piper has enriched the classic repertoire with his *Companion Guide to London* (1964): 'All buses cover the routes in both directions, a fact one may well forget in the heat of the moment'; and the authors of the *Michelin Guide to New York City* (1968) honour old traditions handsomely with their conclusions on the New York subway: 'Riding the subway is an exciting experience for visitors, but daily commuters who have had a chance to try the comforts of the Paris or Montreal metroes would probably prefer to ride on those silent and modern trains equipped with special steel cord tires of French manufacture.'

But generally when despondency impends it is to nineteenth-century practitioners that I turn, and this is largely I think because they are of the railway age, and transport me through their vicarious delights to the lilt of sleeping-car wheels and the clickety-click of the permanent way—only broken by the cries of the *douaniers* at Modane ('British passengers not required to produce passports') or the intrusions of the ticket collector at Wierzbolow ('Passengers are recommended to pay the difference at St. Petersburg between 1st and 2nd class, which is only 7 rs. 84c.'). One of the grandest of the railway manuals was the *Guide to the Great Siberian Railway* (1900), published by the Imperial Ministry of Ways and Communications in an English translation intended to lure English tourists and businessmen along the golden road to Vladivostok. This stands on my shelves in a position pre-ordained: next door to Adam's and Bishop's *Complete Traveler's Guide of the Union and Central Pacific Railroads* (1881), 'The Hand-somest Guide-Book in the World'.

No escape could be more utter than an hour with these two illus-trated books, side by side upon the hearth. Both their worlds have vanished: the Russia of 1900 so tentative, so defensive, so clamped behind the frontispiece of His Imperial Majesty Nicholas Alexan-drovich, Autocrat of All the Russias and Most August President of the Siberian Railway; the America of 1881 so marvellously brash and energetic, so full of hope, so innocently encapsulated in this, 'The Most Complete, Accurate and Reliable Trans-Continental Guide Ever Known'—'far in advance', as Samuel Powell, General Ticket Agent of the Chicago, Burlington and Quincy Railroad, testifies, 'of any other work of similar character that has come to my notice'.

Take the trains themselves, into whose varnished and embossed compartments these volumes so vividly usher us. It is true that palace-car life on the Union Pacific looks more fun, at least in lithograph, with songs at the harmonium, mysterious Indians hovering around the spittoon, and a most comfortable and convenient eating-house to look forward to at Rock Creek, Wyoming. The week's journey from Chicago to the coast may well pass like a flash if, as the book suggests, we 'indulge in social conversation and glee'. But the Great Siberian Railway actually has a Church Car, with icons, tall candles, a priest in attendance and a cross on the roof: and no Pullman could match the listless Chekhovian dignity of the Great Siberian saloon, with its glass-fronted library shelves, its tasselled armchairs, its portraits of eminent railway engineers and its chessmen already laid out for play on the corner table beneath the clock.

From the windows of the Union Pacific one sees feathered Sioux, elks, beautiful cowboys, scenic wonders and the Family Residence of Brigham Young. From the windows of the Great Siberian one looks out upon a morose parade of Yakutsk, Ostyaks and landing-places on the Ob. The hotel at Cheyenne depot is hung with the heads of black-tailed deer, 'all nicely preserved and looking very natural', but the station at Olginskaya looks like the pavilion of some exceptionally prosperous bowling club, or perhaps a small casino. The Union Pacific guide has a picture of a venerable engine-driver leaning from his cab to kiss an infant a whiskery good-bye. The *Guide to the Great Siberian Railway* contains a message from the All Highest: 'Gentlemen! To have begun the construction of the railway line across Siberia is one of the greatest achievements of my never to be forgotten Father. The fulfilment of this essentially peaceful work, entrusted to me by my beloved Father, is my sacred duty and my sincere desire.'

Yet both books are, in their disparate ways, expressions of Manifest Destiny. The aftertaste of such old convictions, so urgent or majestic in their time, now harmless or discredited, is for the real *aficionado* a peculiar delicacy of old guide-books.

*   *   *

Another is a sense of transference, the power Murray and Baedeker possess to deposit you in the shoes of your great-grandparents, to see the world with their eyes, dip into their capacious bags for Gratuities or Cockle's Pills ('if not used by oneself, they are useful to give to servants or villagers'), or make it clear to the manager of the Hotel Dagmar that you will not put up, as so many travellers in Denmark are obliged to, with damp table napkins.

The English guides are best for this. They make one feel gloriously assured. Herr Baedeker can be scathing enough about the performances of Egyptian clowns—'disgracefully insolent'—or the morals of Neapolitan innkeepers—'The traveller is often tempted to doubt whether such a thing as honesty is known here': but for sheer superbia, for the exhilaration of *noblesse oblige*, the English nineteenth-century guide-book stands alone. There are disappointments, of course. T. Bennett in *Handbook for Norway* (1878) tells us abjectly that because so many foolish things are written by British travellers in railway suggestion books, the authorities seldom pay any attention to remarks entered in English: but then Mr. Bennett, the doyen of Norwegian tourism, lives in Christiana himself and is probably demoralized by intimate contact with natives. Far more characteristic is Mr. Hare's Augustan dismissal of Venetian guides: 'All but the most hopelessly imbecile travellers will find them an intolerable nuisance', or Murray's noble reassurance to British visitors in Athens: 'Any Englishman having the usual knowledge of ancient Greek will be able to read the Athenian papers with ease.'

For it is true, I fear, that the best guide-books, like the best travel books, are generally written by resolute outsiders—observers who preserve the integrity of detachment, and write first of all to their own satisfaction. Americans are bad at this, feeling in themselves a necessity to integrate, which is why they so often produce ingratiating guides and ineffable books of travel: but our British forebears, secure in the extraordinary good fortune of their nationality and the inestimable advantage of a classical education, were very good at it indeed. They were seldom so mean as to be curmudgeonly, but they felt no need to be fulsome. This was the Eothen vein, which was worked skilfully into our own times by Robert Byron and Peter Fleming, but which displayed its richest lode in the travel literature of mid-Victorian Britain.

The greatest guide-book of all is Murray's *Handbook for Spain* (1845), which is the masterpiece of Richard Ford, and one of the best books of any kind about Spain. Transference to the plane of this work is the perfect stimulant, for never was there so racy, so exuberant, so learned, so marvellously uninhibited a traveller as Ford. In his company, one feels, nothing can go wrong for long, and boredom is impossible. The Valencians may well be perfidious, vindictive, sullen, mistrustful, fickle, treacherous, smooth, empty of all good, snarling and biting like hyenas and smiling as they murder, but dear Richard's charm will soon win them over: as for the Spanish smuggler, that swaggering MacHeath of Andalusia, a cigar and a *bota* of wine will soon open his heart, and anyway he likes and trusts an Englishman—'not that he won't rob him if in want of cash'.

Ford is often rude, but, because he cares for nobody's opinion, never priggish or patronizing. His exasperations are always redeemed by humour; his admiration is as generous as his contempt is unsparing. One feels in his presence that the best guide-books are far more than informational aides, more even than literature, but are manuals of sensibility. When I travel with Richard Ford, if only in the privacy of my own library, I assume not merely his vision and hearing, but his feelings too: I am brightened in myself by his gaiety, enriched by his scholarship, mellowed by his kindness. Travel in a foreign country, especially perhaps such a country as Spain in the 1840s, should exercise every faculty: like a Finnish sauna or Eng. Lit. at Cambridge, it ought to be an awakening of all our powers, and an invitation to experiences that require no Steamship Reservations or Changes of Train at all.

This is the gift of the best of these English guides: to give to the reader even now something of the potency, the alertness and the dash that went with Victorian England's convictions of merit. There is nothing like it, I find, after the ten o'clock news.

* * *

Yet I cannot deny that half the pleasures of my old guide-books are physical. I love them as objects. I have in my shelves a facsimile edition of Baedeker's English *Guide to Russia*. It is a handsome replica, and provides an unequalled diagram of Russia in the last years of the monarchy: but though I admit it is handy to know that Matins in the English Church at Riga is at 11 a.m., and comforting to be told that the Girls' Friendly Society maintains a hostel in Odessa, still I think I shall always cherish more dearly my original German version of the book, whose pages are yellowing, whose maps are ragged at the edges, and which I bought one icy November morning in the Nevski Prospekt—empty, alas, of the scarlet-liveried carriages and Tartar old-clothes pedlars recommended to me inside.

For all the magic of the old guides cannot be reproduced. It is only partly in their words; the rest is embodied in their smell of age and foreign ink, the suggestion of salt-spray on their bindings, the spindly signatures of their previous owners, or the faded pink Ticket of Admittance, tucked still within the museum itinerary, which, like a madeleine dipped in tea, can evoke so miraculously other times in distant places.

THE CITY-STATE

And on from thence, I misquoted to myself as I boarded the aircraft in Hong Kong, and on from thence to Singapore: and though the Lion City is hardly a garden of the sun, at least it is distinctly golden, and possesses a mingled allure of the rapacious, the aggressive, the repellent and the extraordinary that any true pilgrim would relish. We live in a world of alliances, alignments and conformities: for the professional traveller there is nothing more agreeable than to reach, like the desert caravans of old, a place that is altogether on its own, ramparted, defiant and *sui generis*. Such a place, like it or not, is undeniably the Republic of Singapore. It is like nowhere else. It lives adventurously. It is equally admired and detested. It glitters in the anticipation. It stands on the sea's edge, ostentatiously. It is the last of the city-states—or perhaps, gnomically speaking, the first.

*   *   *

No Florence, though, or Mantua. Flat, steamy, thickly humid, the island lies there in its hot seas, fringed with mangrove swamps, and from the air it looks as it always did, a slightly desperate place that ought to be uninhabited. It looks an invented place, and so of course it is: for it was created by the British virtually out of nothing, to consolidate their command of the eastern trade. Only a handful of Malays, Chinese farmers and peripatetic seamen lived uncomfortably on Singapura when Stamford Raffles bought it from Chief Temonggong and Sultan Tengku Long of Johore: the island was brought to life by the alchemy of Empire.

The artefacts of the British still show down there, adjusting geography as they so often did. There is the Johore Causeway, still the one link with the Malay peninsula, which the imperialists built to connect the island with their protectorates upon the mainland. There is the naval base upon the Johore Strait, one of the last great military works of the British Empire. There the island roads converge, as they do in many another imperial island, upon the sprawl of the seaport around its harbour. There are the jostling sampans still, like a log-jam in the Singapore River, and there are the ranks of ships in the roadsteads, fussed about by launches, tugs and bum-boats, that the magnetism of Empire first attracted to this fulcrum of the eastern seas.

For most Britons of a certain age, I suppose, Singapore remains Raffles's island to this day: but it is poignantly true that although no possession of the old Empire was more dashingly acquired, romantically conceived, or successfully developed, still in historical terms Singapore remains a figure of all that was fustiest and snobbiest in the colonial Empire, all that went with baggy shorts and ridiculous moustaches, with servant problems and Sunday sing-songs at the Seaview, with tennis clubs and beer and meeting for elevenses at Robinson's—with everything that was most bourgeois about the declining Empire, and in the end with everything that was most ineffectual. Singapore was the archetype of Somerset Maugham's Empire, Noel Coward's Empire—an Empire that had lost its purpose, its confidence and its will: when it fell to the Japanese in 1942, in effect the Empire fell too, and the idea of Empire too.

When I landed in Singapore a homing instinct led me direct to the core of this dead colony, the downtown expanse of green called the Padang, and there without surprise I discovered that the imperial ghosts live on. There was the warm nostalgic smell of mown grass. The last post-prandial members of the Singapore Cricket Club were still sitting with their gin-slings on the veranda, white linen hats over their eyes. There stood the spire of the Anglican cathedral, fretted but still handsome in its close, with small Anglican-looking cars parked outside its offices, and large Anglican-looking ladies co-ordinating arrangements in its porch. Ineffably conceited barristers, direct from Lincoln's Inn, adjusted their wing-collars or tilted their wigs beneath the colonnade of the Supreme Court: civil servants with brief-cases hurried preoccupied into the great offices of Government from whose windows, during a century of British rule, expatriate administrators looked out with pride or loathing across the tropic green.

Away to the west, over Anderson Bridge, the lumpish structures of imperial capitalism still breathed the spirit of the thirties, so that I half-expected to see Oxford bags and monocles emerging from their revolving doors, or wives in pink cloche hats dropping in on Reggie. Away to the east stood the glorious palms of Raffles Hotel,

that grand caravanserai of Empire, the Shepheards of the East, where
the Maughams used to drink and the Cowards fizz, where the gin-
sling was invented, where there was a Free Dark Room for Amateur
Photographers, and Hotel Runners Boarded All In-coming Steamers,
where Admiral Skrydloff and the Duke of Newcastle stayed, where
generations of Malayan planters intrigued their leaves away, and not a
few planters' wives began their tearful journeys home to mother.

It is all there still. There are no Britons in those offices of Government. Those barristers are mostly Indian. The Finest Organ in the East
no longer plays for Lady Tumsbury's charity balls at the Victoria
Memorial Hall. The spin-drift ensigns of the regiments have been
removed from the Cathedral. Even Raffles, in an uncharacteristically
philistine moment, recently lowered the ceilings of its vast bedrooms,
where the old iron fans used to creak and swirl through the nights of
exile or ecstasy. Yet those ghosts wander there still, mostly dead but
sometimes alive, and the ethos of the dying Empire, threadbare,
raffish, gone to seed, well-meaning, lingers there forlornly.

It was from the Padang that the humiliated tuans and their wives,
mustered by the Japanese, began their cruel march to Changi Prison
and often to death: and if I closed my eyes, I thought, I could still hear
their voices in the sunshine, courageous or querulous, insisting upon
water for the dogs or bursting bravely into 'There'll Always Be An
England'. The British Empire went out with a whimper, assiduously
though we have disguised the fact even to ourselves, and in Singapore
especially it faded away in pathos—or worse still, bathos, for the
generals were second-rate, the songs were banal, the policies were
ineffectual, and even the courage was less than universal.

I find this mixture very moving—the imperial energies debased and
enervated, like a very exclusive sport when the masses take it over.
Singapore fell partly because its defence was timid and inept, but
partly because its rulers did not wish to put at risk the lives of their
indigenous subjects: it was an attitude flaccid but not altogether
ignoble, and translated to a wider sphere, it meant that the Empire
had outlived itself. My *Whitaker's Almanack* for 1945 records Singapore
as being 'temporarily in hostile Japanese occupation': but though that
'temporarily' proved true, and the British did raise their flag again
above the Padang, still things could never be the same again. The good
of Empire, like the bad, depended upon force and the will to use it:
by 1945 the British had lost that will for ever, and for that matter the
force too.

In a masochistic moment I determined to visit the exact spot where, on 15 February 1942, was sealed the fate of Singapore and thus of the British Empire—which Churchill himself, only a year or two before, had conjectured might last a thousand years. The Japanese had then captured most of the island, but had only penetrated the outskirts of Singapore City: short of fuel and ammunition, they were exerting their will upon the hapless British more by bluff than by superior power. They were on a winning streak, the British unmistakably on a losing: at seven o'clock that evening General Percival, wearing his steel helmet and long shorts, walked along the Bukit Timah road to meet General Yamashita at the Ford Motor Company factory, and surrender Raffles' island to the Great East Asia Co-Prosperity Sphere.

The factory has not much changed since then. The buildings are still modest, low and rather drab, and the man at the gate still raises his barrier with that faintly military manner so characteristic of lesser functionaries under British colonial rule. Inside, the offices have been shifted around somewhat, and separated with glass partitions, and the room in which the surrender was signed has been divided into two. Nevertheless, they said, as they showed me into a fairly gloomy, wood-panelled and teak-furnished executive chamber, this was the very place where the surrender was signed. Even the furniture was the same. Here sat Percival and his three staff officers, hangdog and exhausted, hopelessly, almost obsequiously asking for more time. Here sat the bullish Yamashita in his medal ribbons and open-necked shirt—'All I want to know is, do you surrender unconditionally or not? Yes or no?' The fans whirred heavily above their heads, and as the sun began to set the dim electric lights came on: in the long silences Percival stared helpless at his papers, Yamashita's fingers drummed the table-top. Japanese war correspondents and military photographers jostled all around the table, Yamashita's generals sat impassive beside him. I could see the tired eyes of the British officers, flinching in the flare of the flash-bulbs, as Percival accepted the terms with a limp 'Yes', and the papers were signed—Yamashita in a bold flourish, Percival in a cramped schoolboyish hand with what I would surmise to be a Conway Stewart 2s 6d fountain pen.

I felt ashamed to be there, and sorry, and I wished poor General Percival happier campaigning in his afterlife—'He looked so pale and thin and ill,' said General Yamashita later, before they hanged him for his war crimes. Did many British visitors come to see the room? I asked the Ford people. Not very many, they said, very few in fact:

but seldom a day went by without a coachload of Japanese tourists stopping at the factory gate, while their guide pointed out the historic window, and the Canons clicked.

*   *   *

Singapore is a harbour, and when the British went, the harbour stayed. One afternoon I rented a sampan, and chugged with a couple of friends to an off-shore island called Sakijang Bendera, which looked enticing on the map. It took a long time to get there. The ignition keys were missing. The engine wouldn't start. The boatman remembered some unfinished business on the next pier but one. The sampan, though sturdy, was not swift. Spray got in our eyes, oil got on our skirts, the heat blazed mercilessly down, warming the water like a tepid bath and blurring the horizons in mirage. Once a tropical storm burst violently over us, and sometimes the boatman made despondent grunting noises, as though he wished he had never come.

But this is the best way to experience the harbour of Singapore— sweating, soaked, oiled, delayed, slightly irritated. These are the conditions of the place, and best illustrate its origins and meanings. Raffles chose the island as his new entrepôt because he recognized it as the ideal staging-post on the Oriental shipping routes, commanding the narrow straits by which shipping must pass from the Indian Ocean to the China Sea. Here, 100 miles north of the equator, the Indian, the Chinese and the Polynesian worlds meet, and the great trade routes converge. It is Conrad country, where the seamen of every nation clamber ashore for their pleasure at Connaught Pier, the coasters labour in from Borneo and Java, and the original Bill Bailey ignored all requests to go home from his celebrated bar in Cuppage Road. The average noonday temperature of Singapore is 87° Fahrenheit, and the population is a heady mixture of the races, packed tumultuously around the great port as in a huge bazaar.

All about us, as we proceeded jerkily across the harbour, ships and islands lay: the islands green with palms and mangroves, and suggestive with the remains of fortifications: the ships anchored row by row, like a city of ships, some high in the water, some deep with merchandise, from Monrovia and from Panama, from Liverpool and from Yokohama; and from their rails the wan faces of sailors looked down upon us like prisoners, sometimes offering us a listless wave, or chewing gum like camels. The water was thick and scummy, the ships all looked rusty, it rained again, and when we got to the island an adamant official said we were forbidden to land there, owing to its being a quarantine station for *highly* infectious diseases—'*deadly* diseases, Madam, I cannot allow you to run the risks'. I enjoyed every minute of the trip, and thought it admirably demonstrated for me the brutal continuity of Singapore.

*   *   *

Actually hardly anybody in Singapore seems to think about history at all. The reason for this is that though the Malays originally owned Singapore, the British developed it and the Japanese conquered it, it was always the Chinese who really ran it. Year by year, generation after generation, they drifted down the line of the peninsula from their Chinese homeland, intuitively attracted by the opportunities of Singapore, until they far outnumbered Britons and Malays alike, and provided most of the island's muscles, and much of its brains. The Chinese are not habitually interested in the past, and the result is that Singapore essentially lives for the day, and does not much bother about history. The statues of Raffles and other imperial worthies survive unmolested, but lacklustrely, as though nobody is quite sure who they are: and the Singapore Museum, so painstakingly built up by the imperialists, seems to have fallen into a genteel but unloved decline.

The Chineseness of Singapore is a quality of the overseas Chinese, and thus stands to the central Chinese tradition, I suppose, rather as Australianness stands to England. It is very different from the ethos of Hong Kong, whose citizens stand in everyday contiguity to China, and see the shores and hills of their heartland every day of their lives. Singapore is 1,500 miles from China, and the vast majority of its inhabitants have never set eyes on the country. In Hong Kong one feels China beckoning her children home across the Sham Chun river: in Singapore one senses only the steelier, less emotional genius of China in exile.

China in Singapore is not beautiful. No great monuments give it grandeur. Its architecture is a muddle of styles east, west and un-classifiable. Its faces are, to western eyes, parchments of bland reticence. Its colours are greyish, greenish, wooden, sun-bleached colours. Its shapes are higgledy-piggledy. It seems beyond number and beyond control, yet it seems to move, too, with an inner deliberation, an innate expertise, that gives it an almost conspiratorial air, very different to the jolly push and roguery of Hong Kong.

Three-quarters of Singapore citizens are Chinese, and in effect this is a great Chinese city, one of the greatest. Everything that is most vigorous about it is Chinese-sponsored, from the skyscraper to the corner boutique, from the exquisite cuisine of the great restaurants to the multitudinous eating-stalls which, miraculously as the sun goes down, spring up in the streets and car parks of the city. The grave bewigged judges of the Supreme Court, impeccable though their Oxford English may be, and remote their acquaintance with Peking and Soochow, are really as Chinese as Mao himself. The sampan man in the harbour, though he lives and moves against a background of equatorial sleaziness, is no more than a transplanted junk man from the austere grey Yangtse. Nine of the twelve Cabinet Ministers in the Singapore Government have Chinese names, and even now most Singapore citizens over thirty, say, if you ask them their nationality, will say Hokkien, Cantonese or Hakka.

There is in fact a Chinatown, in the heart of the downtown city. Once it was a racial enclave created by British town planners in the cause of communal harmony; now it is merely a quarter even more thickly Chinese than all the rest. They are going to pull it down soon, for it is old-fashioned, untidy and picturesque, and already its nooks are being whittled away, and its crannies given logic: but I often strolled through it during my stay in Singapore, walking there across the green from Raffles Hotel, and spending an hour or so loitering around the waterfront of the Singapore river, which forms the promenade of Chinatown. Everyone was kind to me, for the Singapore Chinese seem to have, like Scots or Yankees, gentle natures beneath dour fronts, and in the Chinese way nothing is particularly private down there, and nobody minds you poking about.

So I pottered here and there among the go-downs, feeling always the pulse of profit, and I trod the precarious gangplanks to the lighters in the river, and I peered over the shoulders of the tally-men, intent at their ledgers in the shady warehouse doors. It was blazing hot whenever I was there, and all the earnest motion of the waterfront made it seem hotter still: so that often I took a few moments off from my investigations, and sat on a doorstep in the shade, fanning myself with my hat, while the local grandmothers mumbled incoherently but benevolently beside me, and the barefoot children gathered around as for a bedtime story. 'Lady hot?' the passing labourers would say, and sometimes they would answer their own questions with a grin, humping their sacks upon their backs, or staggering beneath the load of a girder—'very hot, too too hot today . . . .'

Behind the waterfront the Chinese do their shopping. Here the food markets sprawl among the narrow streets, and deal in exotica like dried frogs and snake flesh, laid out beneath their tattered awnings in flamboyant exhibition. There are panoramas of fruit, oranges, papayas, rambutans, limes, pears from Japan, apples from South Africa and the legendary durian, which smells so bad and tastes so scrumptious. There are eggs caked in mud, and bundles of dried fish, and indefinable herbs, and vegetables unknown to man, and cages of grasshoppers. The market women eyed me wrinkled and amused as I stood aghast before these marvels, and made witty remarks to each other in Hokkien: but the shoppers spared me hardly a glance, for they were choosing their victuals with a scholarly concentration, calculating the density of turnips, contemplating the specific gravity of carp, comparing the metabolisms of goose liver and pickled crab, before with decisive gestures they solved their several equations, and stuffing liver, noodles, pressed duck and sharks' fins into their blue and yellow plastic shopping bags, hastened home to make the soup.

Though fun for foreigners, little of this is actually remarkable. It is standard Chinadom, more or less, as it exists more or less anywhere in the Chinese world. Singapore Chinatown does have a few distinctive quirks—the ornate caved clubhouses of the hongs, once gangsters' mobs, now charitable societies, or the sad street of the about-to-die, where the withered faces of the terminally sick look wistfully to the street below from their rented chambers above the coffin-shops. Mostly, though, this is a fairly ordinary community of the overseas Chinese. It has the organic strength of the commonplace, and it feels absolutely inextinguishable, as though no natural calamity, no historical force, could ever wrest it from the island, or wrench the go-down capitalists from their abaci upon the quays.

* * *

The classic view of Singapore is from Mount Faber, a hillock which stands to the west of the harbour. Everyone goes up there to see the view. The hill was named for a nineteenth-century colonial engineer, otherwise only remembered for his sensible demand that the Singapore river be deepened, when his bridge over it proved too low to let the lighters through. In British times the indefatigable wives of colonial secretaries and directors of public works came up here to paint their watercolours, and nowadays the practitioners of Tai Chi, the ritual exercises of the Chinese discipline, pursue their craft on the summit.

Not long ago Mount Faber was almost rural, with only a bumpy way
worn to the summit by the wheels of landaus: now there is a tarred
highway to the top, and a dramatic cable-way links it across the water
to the newly developed resort island of Sentosa, on the whole the least
inviting tourist project I know.

When I first went to Singapore it was the Raj that chiefly showed
from Mount Faber, and filled my sketchbook pages, as it had filled
Lady Timsbury's, with its domes and steeples. In those days the Padang
and its buildings looked the embodiment of authority: its law courts
and office blocks were like policemen linking arms to control the
crush of the crowd behind, and keep it off the green. Then the crowd
was about 800,000 strong: today it is more than two million, and
has so overwhelmed that stately cordon that the policemen hardly
show. Dome and portico, Raffles and Empress Place are humiliated by
the thickets and shafts of the new skyscrapers—gleaming, rectangular,
terrifically ostentatious and none more than ten years old. New
Singapore seems to be sprouting there before your eyes, and its
proliferation of gaudy curtain-walls, its frenzy of penthouses and
observation decks, defied my sketchbook pen, and made me turn the
other way in desperation, and attempt a dispirited rendering of Sentosa.

They are a nasty kind of skyscraper—very rich, very arrogant, very
vulgar, more like Centre Point than the Seagram Building. But they
are more than mere show. They truly represent, as potently as the old
Padang, a political energy: the new insular dynamic, born by defiance
out of danger, which has made Singapore something new in the world
for a second time, and created on this steamy island a new kind of state.

*   *   *

When the constituent parts of the British Empire were left to find
their own place in the world, blessed one by one with a grant-in-aid
and a farewell visit from royalty, Singapore was left more in the cold
than most. It existed only as a cog in the imperial machine, one of the
four Straits Settlements which were governed as crown colonies
around the perimeter of the Malay protectorates (the others were
Penang, Malacca and Labuan). It was a predominantly Chinese island
in a region profoundly suspicious of the Chinese, a non-Islamic
community in a strongly Muslim part of the world. Attempts to
incorporate Singapore in the Malaysian Federation soon failed, the
Malaysians having no wish to be dominated by the Singapore Chinese;
relations with the Indonesians to the south were very nearly warlike;

in 1965 Singapore declared itself a sovereign republic, 'founded upon the principles of liberty and justice', with a flag of a crescent moon with five white stars, and the motto 'Let Singapore Flourish'. A city-state was born, recognizably in the tradition of the merchant-princes, with a total area of 225 square miles, but an energy that made it, by 1974, the fourth busiest port on earth.

It is not, I think, an attractive republic, but it certainly has spirit. Though its relations with its neighbours are easier now, it is still a tense, tight little state, with the same prickly and defensive excitement as Israel, say, or Iceland—a backs to the wall, let 'em all come, chips down excitement. It is a noisily opinionated state, strong on hand-outs, short on tact, or sympathy—a harsh and cocky state, setting its own standards, choosing its own styles, and working so hard that its living standards are claimed to be the highest in Asia, excepting only Japan's. There are very few clubs in modern Singapore; there are no beggars at all; the railway trains may not arrive punctually, for they come over the Johore Causeway from Kuala Lumpur and Bangkok, but I am quite sure they *leave* on time.

It is no coincidence that the new Singapore, like the old, is the creation of one man. There is no room here for committee government: until the war Singapore was an absolute dependency of Britain, and the Governor was in effect omnipotent—'Well,' said His Excellency Sir Shenton Thomas, when told that the Japanese Imperial Army had invaded Malaya, 'I suppose you'll shove the little men off!' I never saw Lee Kuan Yew when I was in Singapore, but like everyone else I felt I knew him well, from his frequent appearances on television, his well-known political opinions, and the sensation of his ubiquitous power. Physically, it is true, I sometimes confused him in my mind with Willy Brandt, to whom he bears a paradoxical Orientalized resemblance: but metaphysically I saw him clear, for he is perhaps the last in the line of western-educated Chinese autocrats, a man built for greater power, the commands of armies or the marshalling of provinces, who is obliged by history to channel his brilliant and perhaps bitter abilities into the narrow arena of a state less populous than Wales.

'The first 150 years of Singapore', says a commemorative history published in association with the Singapore International Chamber of Commerce, 'open and close under the aegis of a great man: Raffles . . . pointing the way: Lee Kuan Yew for today.' Connoisseurs of sycophantic history, or for that matter of post-imperial commerce, will recognize the tone of this remark. It is the tone of a wary citizen, brought up in the liberal tradition of the west, who finds himself subject to a very different kind of authority, and is playing it cautiously. I have heard it in many corners of the old Empire, Ghana to St. Lucia, and if I observe that it seldom seems to have done anybody much good for long, I am not implying that Lee Kuan Yew is just another petty despot. He is by all accounts a cultivated and charming man, with a Cambridge law degree and a witty mind: but he is nevertheless, if not actually a dictator, at least an authoritarian, at the head of a one-party state, and in his Singapore you will detect most of dictatorship's symptoms, good, bad and disturbing.

Like many autocracies, Lee Kuan Yew's is very logical. Singapore has no natural resources, except its human ones, and it lives by its abilities. It makes things out of other peoples' substances, it loads and transships other peoples' cargoes, it fuels and mends other peoples' ships and aircraft, it insures and disposes other peoples' goods, it gives advice, it banks money, it shows itself to visitors from elsewhere. Like many another former imperial entrepôt or dockyard—Malta, Gibraltar, Hong Kong—it sets out to perform, as a free-lance, the offices it once performed, as a staff member, for the British Empire. This is a precarious status. Lee Kuan Yew believes that to preserve it, the whole state must be resolutely directed towards a kind of communal expertise. There is no time for argument. There is no room for dilettantism, nostalgia or party politics. Prosperity is the single aim of the state, and it can be retained only by rigorous discipline and specialization, under the unchallenged authority of an intelligent despotism. Political stability, reasons Lee Kuan Yew, equals foreign confidence, equals investment, equals money for all, which is all the average citizen wants of life and statesmanship.

In some ways this is a Puritan ethic, and both Cromwell and Mao would approve of many of Lee Kuan Yew's policies. Singapore is clean, relatively honest, apparently undecadent. Litter on the streets is savagely punished, drugs are mercilessly kept out, the rock culture is pointedly discouraged. Newspapers must toe the official line or disappear, and dissenting politicians too are apt to find themselves in trouble, or even prison. All this makes of course for the usual autocratic drabness. Nothing is more *boring* than a one-party state, and nothing is more dispiriting than to wake up at Raffles Hotel, settling down to papaya, toast and marmalade, and to find that there is nothing to read but the *Straits Times*, a newspaper rather less outspoken than *Little Women*.

Everywhere in Singapore nowadays one feels the imprint of a single and implacable intelligence. At the University the arts faculties are being encouraged to die on their feet, as useless parasites of a technical society. At the cinema black blobs expunge unsuitable passages of film, as messengers of degeneration. At the airport young visitors are to be seen shepherded in embarrassment towards inner chambers, to have their hair cut. Beside the Anderson Bridge a hideous concrete chimera, half-lion, half-dolphin, adequately symbolizes both the republic's self-image and its aesthetic standards. Nothing, one feels in Singapore, is being left to chance: serendipity is the very last of this republic's virtues. Singapore is a living-machine, highly functional, with the ornamentation reduced to a minimum, and an inflexible foreman at the controls.

It is all very deliberate, very rational. Take industry. Since the entrepôt business is always vulnerable, and depends upon the economic circumstances of others, Singapore has deliberately turned itself into a manufacturing state—and not just any old manufactures, but specifically sophisticated products which less highly skilled labour forces cannot manage. Young people are being educated towards this specific end, a new industrial city has been built on the most modern lines in the swamp country of the south-west, and already industry is more important to Singapore than the entrepôt trade of tradition.

Or take congestion. Since the land area is so small, the new Singapore is rebuilding itself on revolutionary lines. It is not simply that buildings are going higher. In Singapore entire social complexes are being concentrated within single blocks, containing not only hundreds of shops, offices, flats, but hotels, theatres, garages, swimming-pools, the whole entity pulled together by the inescapable escalators, perpetually packed and often visible from the street outside, which remain in my mind as the kinetic emblems of the republic. The population is being rehoused in equally concentrated complexes, and so Singapore takes on an altogether new appearance, not quite like anywhere else I know, and more truly futuristic than anywhere else I know.

Or take tourism. This is very important to Singapore, and the Government adeptly adjusts some of its principles to accommodate it, especially as, except for shopping and Sentosa, there is practically nothing in Singapore for a tourist to do. When it comes to tourism Lee Kuan Yew's asceticism is modified, and all is indulgent luxury. There is the customary duty-free shopping, of course, without which no tourist haven can respectably survive. But there is also a carefully cherished ambience of the sybaritic. 'Instant Asia', the local publicists call Singapore, but it is an opulent kind of Asia. There are said to be more first-class hotels on Orange Road, once the epitome of colonial suburbia, than in the whole of Australia, and everywhere the travel agents proliferate, the foreign exchanges thrive, soft music sounds from hotel mezzanines and wildly extravagant foods are served in preposterously garish décors.

It really is a new world—as new as the world that Raffles created, within this same cramped ground of experiment. Singapore's is a purely modern, technological society, without slack or sentiment: semi-communal, half brain-washed, materialist to the point of philistinism, but healthy, rich and enterprising. I expect it will crack one day, like most autocracies, when Lee Kuan Yew finally exceeds himself, succumbs to *folie de grandeur*, grows old or even dies, if death has not been banned in Singapore by then. In the meantime, the republic does not lose a moment. In every corner of Singapore, one feels, at every moment of day or night, the planners are planning, the excavators are churning, the steam-hammers chug and the ideologues prepare their next injunctions—'hard work, thrift and grit', is what the Finance Minister demanded in a recent budget, and Lee Kuan Yew would undoubtedly add discipline too.

*   *   *

I often asked Singapore people if they were happy under this forceful regime, and once one of my hosts asked a similarly simplistic question of me. We were eating a delectable *poh piah* (eggs, squid, shrimp, chilis and mixed greens wrapped up in a thin pancake) at a stall in Hokkien Street, where the night looked down at us through the glare of Chinatown, and the sweating cooks laboured half-naked, towels around their necks, over their blazing stoves. 'You do a lot of travelling,' said my friend, 'so tell me, is Singapore a good idea?'

A good idea? I looked at him blankly, searching in vain for some Confucianist retort, like 'The wise boatman does not measure the current', or 'What use is the scroll without the brush?' I did not know what to say. The impact of the new Singapore is so powerful, so diametrically opposite to the bourgeois pragmatism of the old, that my sensibilities were rather numb. Was it a good idea? I certainly found it stimulating. The neo-Fascist vigour of Singapore is undeniably fun, if only because one feels that despite that chaste veneer it is fundamentally amoral. The futuristic imagination of the place is undeniably exciting. I myself rather relish that sense of zealous and unswerving purpose, not fortunately having to share the purpose myself. I find Lee Kuan Yew vicariously attractive as a person, but then I am often attracted by cultured authoritarianism. Singapore is excellent as theatre, if rather tedious as real life.

But as to the idea of it, I felt disqualified to judge. Though I am by no means an addict of universal democracy, and recognize that our own dear Empire was at least as despotic as Lee Kuan Yew, still I am too much a child of my time and my background to enjoy the taste of autocracy. I believe in man's full and free self-expression. But even as I thought over my reply, I began to feel like an old-school music-lover trying to come to terms with electronic music. Could I be behind the times, in so distrusting the idea? Was this ruthless specialization, this cutting away of dead wood, this discarding of wasted energies, necessary for human survival? Could Lee Kuan Yew be right, in claiming that in Singapore at least, the rich man was happier than the free? How long would you pine for liberty if you had never sampled it?

Twice in a single journey I had been tempted towards these heresies —once looking across the Chinese frontier from Hong Kong, and now toying with my *poh piah* in Hokkien Street. It was not because I was weak in my allegiances: it was because I felt I was experiencing, if only vicariously, something new in the world—a new energy of the east with which, sooner or later, the western peoples will come to grips, if not physically, at least philosophically. It is a sort of mystic materialism, a compelling marriage between principle and technique which neither capitalism nor Soviet Communism seems to me to have achieved.

The great tourist experience of Singapore used to be a visit to Change Alley, the dark covered bazaar, hardly wide enough to stretch one's arms in, through whose gauntlet of Indian shopkeepers and money-changers generations of sailors and globe-trotters picked their bemused and gullible way. I did it once or twice for old times' sakes, stepping into the alley's shadows out of the glare and hustle of the quays, and enduring once more the immemorial banter of the bazaars, that leitmotiv of Empire. 'You wanta change money? You want souvenirs? Look lady, very good silk, real silk. Where you from? You got dollars? You got pounds? Look here, very cheap—come and look, no need to buy, have a cup of coffee with my father!'

Nowadays, though, the excitement of Change Alley comes at the far end of it, where it debouches into Raffles Place. Half-way through I was tempted sometimes to think that nothing changes in the Orient after all, or ever will: but the moment I emerged from that clamorous trap, and saw as in fantasy the new towers of Singapore shining in the sunshine, then I knew I was seeing something new in the world: the city-state, within its island ramparts, brazen and self-assured. It was like emerging from a tunnel under the walls, to surface within some extra-territorial civilization, where everything was shinier and brassier than life, and new kinds of people were genetically reared.

I knew my reactions then. Let me out! I cried in my waking dream. Let me out! Where's Reggie?

ON THE CONFEDERATION SPECIAL

In Toronto once, searching for a theme to illustrate the condition of British Canada in the 1920s, I came across the Reverend Dr. S. W. Fallis, a well-known United Church divine of the day. He did not at once endear himself to me, for he glared at me rather accusatorily from his ill-printed photograph, as though he expected the worst of me, but he did seem splendidly representative of his place and period.

Solid but pasty of feature, bland, broad-jawed, patently as pious as he
was patriotic, he looked an authentic Anglo-Canadian from the days
when British Canadians thought of themselves as British first, Canadians second. Just my man, I said to myself beneath my breath, and
investigated further.

Dr. Fallis (pronounced, luckily, Follis) was the publisher of an
influential United Church magazine, the *New Outlook*, and in 1927
he determined to make a grand celebratory gesture to mark the
Diamond Jubilee of Canadian Federation—sixty years, that was, of
Canadian nationhood. He invited his readers to join him upon a train
journey between two of the staunchest centres of Canadian life,
Toronto in the east, Calgary in the west, to commemorate not only
the continuing Britishness of Canada, but also its noble unity. Dr.
Fallis himself would act as Conductor of the Tour. The response was
gratifying, readers from every province applying for tickets, and Dr.
Fallis accordingly chartered a train, the *New Outlook* Confederation
Special, from the Canadian Pacific Railway. He printed special travel
brochures, he arranged for reports to be sent back to the *New Outlook*,
he ordered commemorative badges and hat-ribbons, and he instructed
his party to assemble at Toronto North railway station at 12 noon
sharp on Saturday, 25 June 1927.

This was just my cup of tea. Severe though Dr. Fallis looked, I
decided to join his party in spirit, and make the journey across Canada
myself in the tracks of the Confederation Special—'a wonderfully
satisfying holiday', the *New Outlook* said it would be, 'after a quarter-
century of work in Church, Sunday School and on the farm'.

*   *   *

On the Friday the eager excursionists inspected Toronto itself, 'the
Queen City'. In 1927 this was still truly the British metropolis of North
America—deliberately and self-consciously so, for it had to resist the
rivalries and magnetisms of Montreal one way, Detroit the other. It
was already caught up in that enervating tangle of the Canadian
spirit called the Search for Identity, and was still in an assertive phase
of the neurosis—Union Jacks all over the place, knighted drapers on
charitable committees, the *Globe* reverberatingly imperialist and the
Lieutenant-Governor's mansion rigid with protocol and royal portraits.

Predisposed though the travellers undoubtedly were towards these
splendours, for they were mostly Scots, they can hardly have found
much to excite them as they walked through Toronto that afternoon.

Drear but pompous the city straggled down to its pallid lake, and the grid streets of downtown seemed to fade from sheer lack of spirit into the suburbs of the north. There was the statutory Anglican cathedral, of course, and the University stood ineffably Oxbridge in its green, and here and there neo-classic palaces of commerce or finance loomed slightly embarrassed at intersections. Nobody, though, could call it a handsome city. It looked more or less like a bit of Birmingham, straightened out, drained of bawdy and homogenized—'a nest', suggested the local writer Jesse Edgar Middleton cosily, or perhaps despairingly, 'of British-thinking, British-acting people'.

It was true that the policemen wore bobby's helmets, and that Lord Bessborough, later Governor-General of Canada, once described Toronto as understanding two things perfectly—'the British Empire and a good horse'. In fact, though, by 1927 Toronto was willy-nilly diverging from its British patterns. For one thing it was far richer than any comparable British city of the homeland. It had far more cars, and many more telephones, and its commerce was run with more push and gusto. The Royal York Hotel, under construction on Front Street, was announced as the Biggest Hotel in the British Empire, and the new Union Station would be perhaps the grandest railway station (though it took so long to get the tracks into it that Will Rogers called it the only station the trains couldn't find).

More telling, though, was the feeling that Toronto's Britishness had to it an air of parody—that first symptom of declining assurance. There was something comic to a civic aristocracy, rich, titled and intensely grand, so inescapably bourgeois as Toronto's. There was something forlorn to the pageantry of the Toronto Scottish, wildly panoplied in all the paraphernalia of their tradition, but bereft of the true Scottish cragginess, too pale, too pudgy. Unquestionably the leading citizen of Toronto in the 1920s was Sir Henry Mill Pellatt, a fervently imperialist financier twice as British as John Bull. His vast Balmoralesque castle on the city's outskirts, Casa Loma, was big enough for his entire militia regiment to parade in his cellars, and was intended specifically for the hospitality of visiting British monarchs: but it succeeded only in becoming a snigger for visiting sophisticates (and is now reduced to that last indignity for noble follies, operation as a tourist spectacle by Kiwanis).

This was the innate weakness of Toronto, never to be overcome—its half-wayness, its hybrid kind, which flattened the impact of its energies and blunted its confidence. It could not find itself, because its loyalties, models and rivalries were all at odds. Gaily though the ferries chugged back and forth to the island pleasure-grounds—bravely though the Canadian National Exhibition Buildings, Largest in the Empire, stood there in the June sunshine—gloriously though Casa Loma towered battlemented over the escarpment—still even those hopeful excursionists, Conductor at their head, must sometimes have sensed the pathos of Toronto. (It is inescapable still, just as the genius of Canada remains essentially a deflationary genius. When they had a competition to name Canada's first space satellite, the poet Leonard Cohen thought that even this prodigy should reflect the Canadian nature. They should call it, he suggested, *Ralph*.)

*   *   *

Still, we assembled in high spirits at the station, Dr. Fallis, his excursionists and I—anticipating an experience, said the *New Outlook*, like that of the Queen of Sheba, 'who had heard of Solomon's glory but who, on seeing the reality, confessed that the half had not been told her'. The Confederation Special awaited us spanking at the platform—nine sleepers, two dining cars, a tourist car, an observation car and a baggage car, headed by one of those ferociously complex locomotives, black and multitudinously pistoned, which were, so to speak, the Canadian satellites of their day (though oddly enough the practice of naming them never caught on). The engine hissed portentously; the stewards stood smiling at their carriage doors, with their little portable steps; our Conductor distributed buttons and hat-ribbons; promptly at 12.50, to a promising aroma of soup from the diners, the train, 'valued at more than a million dollars', steamed out of Toronto for the Land of Promise.

It was no mere whim that had led Dr. Fallis to celebrate the Jubilee with a train ride. The C.P.R. was the true begetter of Canadian nationhood. By binding the nation coast to coast it had not only linked the separate provinces physically, but had helped to counter the longitudinal pull of the explicit American republic beyond the border, and the centrifugal push of the implicit French republic within. What was more, by extending itself still further in steamship services across the Atlantic and Pacific, the C.P.R. had consolidated Canada's position in the British Empire, and made her feel part of a super-Power herself.

Like the leys and cross-tracks of prehistoric man, the railway had acquired a symbolic, almost a mystic meaning. Its reconciling function was only illustrative of Canada's special status among the nations. The twentieth century, Canadians had been told, would be Canada's, but they did not interpret this prophecy in any bombastic sense. They would be rich, but they would be good. They would be American in vivacity and inventiveness, but British in style and conscience. They would cherish what was worthy in the tradition of the Motherland (as they habitually called it then), and discard what was unfair. Like the smooth tracks of the C.P.R., binding with steel and Brown Windsor prairie and forest, Rockies and Atlantic shore, they would stand as benevolent intermediaries between the races, the continents, the centuries. Canada had been given, said *New Outlook*, that week, 'a great and significant place in more than human schemes and planning'.

So, as the great engine steamed through Ontario, into Manitoba, it was with awe that the excursionists watched their Canada pass by. The station names paraded, Missanabie and White River, Heron Bay and Marathon, with an almost biblical solemnity. The gentle thumping of the wheels upon the track was like the rhythm of prayer. On the Sunday morning, when the train was somewhere in the waste land called Lake of the Woods, where moose sometimes peered myopically through the larches, and fishermen in bark canoes paddled silently through the dark still waters—as the train puffed through that wilderness the Reverend H. V. Ellison of Little Current, Ontario, with a party of choristers, passed through the train singing inspiring songs. At Nipigon, by Red Rock, a service was held beside the track, an orchestra having assembled there to play the hymns, and at Port Arthur all the clergymen in the party fanned out to preach sermons in the local United Church chapels.

There was nothing incongruous to this religiosity. British Canada was a very religious place. Its tone had been set by gentlemanly British soldiers and administrators, who believed in *mens sana in corpore sano*, and Scottish Calvinist settlers, who believed in God. Indeed it was this vigorous Christian air, this respect for law, order and due authority, which chiefly differentiated Canada from the United States. The frontier that divided them was artificial, but they were recognizably different in ethos. To the south were gangsters, crooked judges, Indian wars and whiskey peddlers: to the north were Mounties, the Honourable Company, Dr. Fallis and King George V. The American road to the west was beset by war, lust and mayhem: here north of the border one travelled more genteelly, via Canadian Pacific, with Scots, pastors and honest policemen all along the track.

This was the Canadian image, and in general the world accepted it,

with reservations. Canada was certainly respected, but she fired no
ecstasy. The price of goodness was ennui. She was a country without
glamour, wrote John Buchan, presently to become her Governor-
General. She was alive but not kicking, thought Rupert Brooke. The
inconceivable spaces of Canada, which Canadians liked to think
emblematic of their boundless potential, seemed to all too many
foreigners interminably tedious, and the good sense of it all, the de-
corum, seemed to lack spice or fizz. 'A community of moderationists',
is how one Canadian publicist phrased it—and that, sad to say, was
half the trouble.

*   *   *

Nevertheless the further west they travelled, the more excited the
excursionists were by the spectacle outside their windows. There were
the immense grain elevators of Thunder Bay, the biggest in the world,
the true granary of the British Empire and one of the undeniable
power factors of the twentieth century. There were the tremendous
wheat and cattle lands of the prairies, mile after mile of growing
wealth, in whose barns stood the most modern reapers, binders and
harvesters, and in whose garages the very latest Packards, Fords and
Essexes lay complacent. As they drove into Winnipeg Dr. Fallis
himself, 'an experienced autoist', stepped into overalls and drove the
engine himself, as if to symbolize their arrival in those lands of youth,
vigour and panache.

Here was the excitement of Canada, such as it was: its newness,
its brawn, the God-given wealth which expressed itself not only in
wheat and shorthorns, but already in the first oil-wells of the western
fields. Out here Canada's extremes of climate, which merely made
Toronto uncomfortable, gave to life an element of theatre. The summer could be dramatic enough, and often the travellers sweltered in
their compartments, when the train stopped in sudden silence at some
prairie halt, and the sun probed relentlessly through the chinks of their
window-blinds, and made the corrugated iron of the station shanties
shimmer and blur in the heat: but it was the winter that really counted.
In the winter the West became terribly but grandly superlative. When
the Canadians put on their fur coats and astrakhan hats, when they
pulled out their sledges from the back shed, when the snow lay feet
deep through the forests, and the conifers drooped and creaked with
the weight of it—when the fish lay embalmed in their frozen lakes,
and a man could get frostbitten crossing a village street—when the

ice-grey skies of winter, like gun-metal, lay glowering and magnificent over the prairies, then for a few months every year Canada acquired an identity despite herself, and foreigners marvelled at last at her power and grandeur, and wondered why on earth anyone wanted to live there.

Space and history, heat and cold, the Bible, the great railway—all these elements, glimpsed or imagined in the cars of the Confederation Special, made the Canadians what they were, and gave truth to Dr. Fallis's conception of a jubilee binge. They were truly living the meaning of Canada, as they puffed westward: and perhaps it was allegorically proper, too, that their Conductor himself, experienced autoist that he was, found himself involved in an unexplained motor accident during a stop in Jasper National Park, and had to make his own way, dashingly bandaged I hope, through the foothills to Calgary.

* * *

Through it all the excursionists had been warmly conscious that they were in *British* Canada. Quebec and its grievances seemed far away, they seldom heard a word of French, and all along the route familiar manners greeted them. This was after all an imperial occasion, and if the Confederation of 1867 had in principle bonded French and British Canada into equality, there was no denying that in practice the British were somewhat more equal than the French. This was only right. Canada's good purposes could best be achieved within that wider brotherhood, the Empire, and nobody could dispute the Britishness of that.

If Toronto had exemplified the stability and continuity of that Empire, Calgary was held by Canadians to represent its frontier spirit. Calgary was as British as the Queen City, but in a different kind—a more patrician kind in fact, though Sir Henry Pellatt might resist the claim. It was essentially a cow-town, dependent upon the great ranches which surrounded it, and the ranchers gave to it some of the spacious free-and-easy style that characterized Wyoming or Montana south of the frontier. As a matter of fact many of the more stylish ranchers were originally American, having crossed the border when land was cheap or free in Canada, but by now they had mostly been satisfactorily Canadianized—which is to say they read the *Calgary Herald* in the Ranchmen's Club, and sent their wives to call upon Lady Lougheed.

The Confederation Special was boisterously welcomed at Calgary station. Half Calgary society seemed to be there, the men bold in wide-brimmed western Stetsons, the women dashing in last year's cloches, and the excursionists were glad they had kept their buttons and ribbons, if only not to be out-coloured. The Mayor himself swept them off to a welcoming banquet at the Palliser Hotel, where Dr. Fallis, gallantly overcoming his mishap, made a speech 'on a high plane, both educational and inspirational': and many members of the Ranchmen's Club were there too, and all the local church dignitaries, except some of the Methodists, and many worthies of bench, bank, bar and surgery. The Palliser was 'universally recognized as the finest city hotel between Winnipeg and Vancouver', and did the excursionists proud, if not with wine from its Celebrated Cellars, at least with red Alberta Beef.

When they emerged from the hotel, which looked like a pair of upturned boot boxes beside the railway tracks, they found that the southern sky was a blaze of flickering red, like a violent aurora. It was the glow of the burning gases from the Turner Valley oil-field, and it hung there like a banner over the prairie, a blazon of wealth to come. Calgary was like that. If it was less flamboyant than the cities of the American West, it was far bolder than Toronto. It was English rather than Scottish, and it was less inhibited or restrained, more showy, more responsive. I dare say some of the travellers found it a little brash, but only in a boyish and endearing way. They were not taken to the red light district beyond Centre Street, where the cow-hands and riggers found their comforts, they ventured only into the more decorous corners of Chinatown, where the gambling did not show, and some of them even bought Stetson hats for themselves, to salute the cheerful *genius loci*.

Toronto stood recognizably for Empire; Calgary did not stand for anything much, except personal opportunity, but it did still smack of the pioneers. Its main highways were still called trails, and there were citizens alive who remembered the signing of the original treaty, No. 7, with the Indians of the region—Black Blood, Piegan, Sarcee, who still lived docile in their reservation down the Sarcee Trail, and were still paid five dollars a head annually in Government stipends, 'for as long as the sun shines, the grass grows and the rivers run'. Indians still loitered in the city streets, and sometimes gipsies camped down by the river, and cowboys clattered ostentatiously in from the ranch, and Hutterite Anabaptists, in cotton bonnets and black Ukrainian hats, came in by wagon from their communes in the prairie. Calgary was not much to look at—a few dowdy office blocks, railway sheds, cattle yards, a rim of residential suburbs, the Pallisser—but it did have variety.

It had its snobberies too, of course—every imperial town did. The posh families of Calgary—the Hulls, the Lougheeds, the Burns—lived in enfilade, so to speak, south of the railway tracks, training their guns upon each other and upon all visiting celebrities. English values still counted in Alberta—EARL OF CADOGAN BANKRUPT AGAIN, said a headline in the *Herald* during the excursionists' visit—and Old Country cricket was a regular feature of the paper. But far more than Toronto, Calgary, like Australia or New Zealand, represented an altogether new start for people of British stock. Here land was still to be had, opportunity was in the very air, and nothing seemed impossible.

As it happens the Canadian West was, at that moment, enduring a slump, but the Calgary *instinct* was for success. That blaze in the sky was true. Already the Stampede, that grand jamboree of the prairies, was the great event of the Calgary year, and its slogan for 1927 was 'The Lid Is Off'. Toronto might seem a substitute for older societies, but Calgary was more like an alternative. It did not compete, it did not pretend, it was something different in kind. Like most of the Empire's frontier towns, even in the 1920s, it was bursting with optimism, and its occasional gestures of mock-Tudor or hierarchy seemed to be throw-away signs, not to be taken too seriously. The future was not an extension of the Motherland's future, but was Calgary's own. As the city signs say to this day, 'The Car Park Is Temporarily Full'—and in that Temporarily, Calgary speaks.

Yet still the British restraint, the sense of order, distinguished it from the lawless cattle-towns of the American legend. That very Sunday there was a great Patriotic Service at the Knox Church—subject, 'Our Glorious Heritage'—at which Mrs. K. Robinson sang 'Land of Hope and Glory' assisted by Mr. Rimanoczy upon the violin. The excursionists, for all the flair and swank of Calgary, felt themselves still at home, and it was a fitting climax to their symbolic journey when Dr. Fallis led them all across the brown and tufty Elbow, a truly Canadian stream, to plant a commemorative tree in the grounds of Hillhurst United Church, up towards the Crowchild Trail. It was a cotton-wood tree, that most Canadian of poplars; Mr. Fallis planted it with pride, and called it Confederation Tree, before leading his companions back to the railway station for a farewell dinner on the train (Crème Victoria, British Columbia Salmon, Egg Custard with Stewed Plums).

*　　*　　*

Faithfully I had followed the *New Outlook* Confederation Special on its long journey, and affectionately I said good-bye to my fellow travellers and took the evening flight to New York. In their footsteps I had wandered the streets of Toronto, physically transformed now with skyscrapers and Ethnics (as the more Canadians call their more immigranty immigrants), metaphysically much the same. I had lazed happily across Canada on the Canadian Pacific, its track rather bumpier nowadays, but its stewards still courteous and its plums still stewed. I had arrived at Calgary in the weeks before the Stampede, and found the excited city buoyant as ever, and crowned now with one of those tight and soaring clusters of skyscrapers, rising like a mirage from the flat-land, which seem to me, after the towered ridges of Castile, the most thrilling of all city silhouettes.

And I had gone home, as they did, thinking that all in all, by and large, the Canada that Empire created was something to be proud of after all: a dullish country perhaps, and too big by half, but still retaining, to this very day, the sense of innocence which had guided the Conductor and his congregationalists so guilelessly across the prairies half a century ago. I am sorry to have to report that the Confederation Tree was chopped down in the course of church extensions in the 1940s: but Dr. Fallis himself still looks at me as I write, and into his eyes there has now crept, I think, a slightly more approving look—as though, flippant though as I often was, and distressingly inattentive during his speech at the Pallisser banquet, still he has hopes that I may have benefited from the journey.

ON WATERINESS

Among the midnight disturbances that beset the traveller—the reverberation of gear-changes, the clanking of shunted railway-wagons, the dawn garbage trucks, the Last Waltz, the muffled announcement of Flight 538 to Georgetown—among them all, one generic noise offers only solace. It is the sound of water outside one's bedroom window.

Sometimes, in old and elaborate city centres, it speaks of Bernini or Lescot, ancient conduits spouting through sculptured allegory into sentimental pools. Sometimes, on Atlantic shores, it suggests the secret convoys of the sea-trout, upstream through the darkness to hereditary mountain lakes. It may be only the splash of an ornamental runnel in a garden. It may be the terrific cycle of the ocean surf, the succession of thunder, suck and warning silence that gives an unforgettable rhythm to a tropical insomnia.

Whatever its origin, for some of us that intimation of water is a necessary dimension of travel. We may be bored to distraction by scorched posh beaches, we may prefer five crowded hours on a jumbo jet to an age without a name on a cruise ship, but our instinct leads always, wherever we are, like lemmings to the water's edge. It offers a reassurance, perhaps, of nature's dignity. It reminds us that the seas, lakes and rivers have no parking meters still, that the fish are masters of their own migrations, and that somewhere beyond our credit-card conformities, somewhere out there at the end of the pier, grand, green or fragrant things are always happening.

* * *

The waters of the world are sovereign Powers. We may pollute them, dam them or divert them, but they remain beyond our degradation. They are better and older than us. John Burns the radical was right, when he called the Thames 'liquid 'istory'. Many a politician, withdrawing to the Commons terrace or the Kennedy Center balcony from the heady puerilities of debate, must have been sobered into wiser judgement by the dark calm flow of the river below, and there are places in the world where this partnership of the water, at once aesthetic and functional, sets the whole tone of a society, and gives it the particular steady assurance that goes with an organic purpose.

Take, for example, the Mississippi. Abraham Lincoln thought it the most powerful force on earth, and certainly its progress through the American South is masterful more than slavish. Its yellowish muddy motion there, and the endless traffic of the river-craft through its shoals and cut-offs, still dictates the character of the country along its banks; and nothing in travel is more satisfying than to leave your car in a cotton-field of Arkansas or Tennessee, scramble to the ridge of the dusty levee, and discover the great river there at your feet, with the long line of a tow thudding its way to Vicksburg or New Orleans— the radar twirling on its wheelhouse, the sun glinting on its paintwork, and the off-duty crew stripped to the virile waist with mugs of coffee around the galley door.

Or think of a city like Singapore. It is not the most beautiful of towns, but because of the water that is its *raison d'être*, it is one of the most formidable. It was built to a purpose, designed for a trade, and it lives by the sea. Its prospect is the Strait, looking across to Sumatra and the archipelago, and littered with tangled melancholy islands. Its promenade is the waterfront, intermittently dressed up with esplanades and monuments, but in essence a working quay. Everywhere the sea seeps through Singapore, in canals and backwaters and crowded wharfs, and always in the roadsteads lie the ships that are its familiars— opulent tankers from the west—shambled coasters from the island trade—junks, dhows, Malay schooners, warships—and all those myriad bum-boats, ferry-boats, rafts, punts, lighters and antique company launches which seem, in all such Oriental water-cities, never actually to have been constructed, but simply to have been washed up and encrusted on the land's edge, like oysters.

*   *   *

The rush of water is a traveller's elixir! Nothing can beat one of the great waterfalls, when it comes to the exhilaration of foreign travel. At Tisisat, on the Blue Nile below Lake Tana, you may sit meditatively beneath a gourd beside the water's turmoil, lolloped about by occasional baboons, interrogated sometimes by courteous tribesmen, and feeling like one of those distant poised figures in the background of explorers' engravings. At Tequendama in Colombia, on the other hand, you may feel yourself physically shaken by the force of the water—more an eruption than a fall, as though some hidden giant has been blocking the Rio Bogota with his thumb, like a boy with a bath tap. And undiminished remains the marvel of those tremendous cousins of the spectacular, Niagara and Victoria, the touch of whose spray upon one's cheek can still give the most blasé wanderer a sense of complacency.

At another level of excitement there is the joy of a fast river rushing immediately beside your sleeping quarters—a delight which Frank Lloyd Wright tried to reproduce in architecture, and which can give an extra fizz to every awakening. There is an inn on the French side of the Pyrenees, in the Basque village of St. Étienne-de-Baigorry, which perfectly expresses this stimulation for me. The river Nive rushes furiously past this inn, separated from its bedrooms only by a little terrace for eating *truite au bleu* upon, and filling the whole hostelry with its enthusiasm.

I stayed there once, and all day long, up to their thighs in the shaly mountain water beside the inn, an exquisite middle-aged French couple silently fly-fished: he unshakeably urbane with his pipe in his mouth, she miraculously unruffled, as vivid and intense as the river itself, as it pursued its headlong way towards the Bay of Biscay. They never caught a thing, but their failure was wonderfully stylish.

* * *

Often just the presence of water is enough—motionless, inaudible, perhaps even out of sight but for the special washed texture of sea air. For me even Delphi would lose half its mystery without that glorious blue remembrance of the sea far below at Itea, with its cruise-ship riding at anchor in the bay, and its vision of heroes and sea-nymphs.

Wherever mountains touch the sea, or are tipped with high silent lakes, they acquire an altogether different kind of magic: in Norway where the fjords creep into the hills for shelter, in Iceland where the volcano Hekla smokes villainously above an icy ocean, among the memsahib's houseboats in Kashmir or best of all in Wales, where the allegorical hills of Snowdonia stand lapped in legend above Cardigan Bay—'There is no corner of Europe that I know', Belloc once wrote, 'which so moves me with the awe and majesty of great things as does this mass of the northern Welsh mountains seen from this corner of their silent sea.'

Nowhere is water's presence more ennobling than it is in New York, a sea-city that has forgotten its origins. There are days when almost everyone seems to be miserable in New York, if only in awful fits and starts: but when the shopkeepers are at their rudest, the traffic jams at their cruellest, the head waiters at their most preposterous, the tycoons at their least sincere, when the whole of Manhattan seems distorted with violence, dirt and disillusion—even then you have only to ride an elevator to the top of any skyscraper, and there on the edge of the city you will see the waters of New York Bay, that grandest lagoon of the New World, spanned by the slender blue steel of the Verrazano Bridge and traversed with majestic sagacity by the ships of the world.

*   *   *

And there are some places where the water is more than just a consolation, an antidote or a mechanism, but supplies something like an ideology. These are the water-civilizations, and there to the delights of ear and eye are added extra insubstantial satisfactions, sensual but profound, which can sometimes make a journey a fulfilment.

Among the water-reflections of Venice I have often felt this grace, as my small boat has taken me warily from one side of the city to the other, down back-canals evocative with age and rot and dampness, past hidden water-basins and busy shopping arcades above—beneath a hundred high-arched bridges, through the shadows of portentous palaces—sidelong between the dustbin barges and the *vaporetti*, boldly across the Grand Canal—until at last we chug beneath the Bridge of Sighs and I find myself in the Basin of St. Mark's, still to my mind the supreme spectacle of travel, where the lagoon seems to dance before my prow, the tankers tread grandly past Giudecca, and the whole panorama is radiant with the life and light of the sea.

But I have felt it even more suggestively, this limpid, liquid quality of a civilization, in the island of Japan. Everything that is most beautiful about that tantalizing country seems to me of a watery beauty. I think of fragile cedar pavilions balconied beside pools, and shrines rising strangely out of sea-shallows. I remember wooded islands in mountain lakes, and neat little coloured ducks in stone-slabbed castle moats. And at night sometimes, between the clatter of the cutlery and the unidentifiable recurrent hum from somewhere behind the wardrobe, I hear in my imagination the soft hollow plonk of the deer-scarers—

through whose wooden channels a trickle of water flows perpetually backwards and forwards, throwing the little instrument from one balance to the other through the darkness, to create that gentle water-percussion of Kyoto, and keep the timid herds out of the moss-garden.

A NORTHERN PRODIGY

The City Fathers of Edinburgh, surveying their cramped medieval city in the second half of the eighteenth century, and contemplating the splendours of the English Age of Reason, resolved to build a New Town of their own, parallel with the Old. Draining an inconvenient loch, and placing the project in the hands of an enlightened local architect, they were presently gratified to find themselves possessors of one of Europe's most celebrated city systems, as different from their insanitary old hilltop town as *pâté de foie gras*, say, from haggis. Its shopping streets were logical and spacious. Its residential crescents and terraces were handsome and convenient. Now and then it opened into a square, to give light and focus to its pattern, and here and there it unfolded into a pleasant garden. It was very soon filled with philosophers, surgeons, cultivated merchants, modernist clergymen and highly respectable shopkeepers: for above all the New Town of Edinburgh was a *civilized* place, governed by the rules of reasonable conduct, emancipated from the instincts and superstitions of the past.

It is there still fine as ever, visited frequently by aspirant civic reformers, written about by scholarly sociologists and inhabited even now by professors and men of gentlemanly substance. Yet for me the most exciting moment of the New Town occurs when, walking up the gentle slope of Duke Street into St. Andrew Square, I cross the hump and see there before me, framed between the ordered structures of the New Town, the savage black mass of the Old. Nothing could be more dramatic. High on its hill the original Edinburgh stands, and it looks all black. There is the black wall of a fortress. There are black spires and towers. Tall black tenements clamber up the hillside, and the hill itself looks blackened too, as though it has been stained by centuries of smoke and grime. It looks a terrible, majestic, compelling place up there, old as sin and proud as Lucifer. Below the elegant men of reason stroll: up there is Auld Reekie, 'Old Smoky', an ancient prodigy of the north.

*   *   *

For a thousand years at least the whole of Edinburgh was confined within the high ridge of the Old Town, and though it has long since extended north and south, beyond the New Town to the Firth of Forth, beyond the humdrum southern suburbs towards the Braid Hills, still the entire experience of the city is dominated by that old presence on the hill.

Let us wander down the long cobbled street that runs along the ridge, and is called the Royal Mile. It is a medieval street, cloistered against the bitter Scottish winds, whose high small-windowed buildings, towering on either side, have a cold, shuttered, winter look to them, and whose narrow wynds, running away down the hillside, are so stony, narrow and higgledy-piggledy, so secretive and shadowy, so greenless, that they could be nowhere else in the world but Edinburgh.

At one end of the Royal Mile stands the castle on its rock; at the other end is a royal palace; half-way down is the principal shrine of an independent Christian church; nearby is the headquarters of a unique legal system. We are in a capital city.

Capital of what? Not exactly of a sovereign state, for the Scottish monarchs forfeited their sovereignty 300 years ago, and the Scottish ruling class abdicated its rights. Nor exactly of a culture, for nowadays the Scottish civilization is in most respects identical with the English, having lost its language almost entirely, and its literature very nearly. No, Edinburgh is a capital of a more nebulous but perhaps more resilient kind: the capital of an idea. It was Scott Fitzgerald who once said that France was a nation, England a people, but that America possessed the quality of an idea: but scarcely less potent and evocative is the idea of Scotland—which, translated into stone, memory and sweep of sky, is the true meaning of Edinburgh.

Look around you now, down the long expanse of the Royal Mile, and the Scottishness of the scene is almost tangible. Here walk the great men of the idea, Knox the reformer, Scott the novelist, Burns the poet, Robert Louis Stevenson, Bonnie Prince Charlie—charismatic figures every one, at least in death, and all of them once familiar characters of this famous street. In these narrow and unsavoury courts, reeking then of carrion and excrement, haunted by drunks and beggars, generations of Scottish thinkers disputed their theories of faith, medicine or human rights over drams of malt and tankards of Edinburgh ale. At one end of the street the Scottish monarchs presided over their curious court, half exquisite, half barbaric, graced by the urbane French visitors of the Auld Alliance, eerily serenaded by wild pipers from the mountains. At the other end the Scottish pipers stood guard over their heritage, cap-à-pie in the crannies of the fortress like rock-creatures, and periodically letting off blasts, in warning or in celebration, from their grand old castle cannon, Mons Meg.

That power of Scottishness remains. They no longer speak Gaelic in the Royal Mile, except on Sundays in the Gaelic church below the castle: but they certainly speak Scottish, that extraordinary distortion of the English language, tangled about with 'Ochs' and 'Ays' and 'Wees', which strikes the visitor as some kind of hoodwink parody, but which is truly the Scotsman's everyday medium of discourse. They no longer empty their chamber-pots out of the upper windows, to the old Franco-Scottish cry of 'Gardyloo!' or project their vile scurrilities through the echoing courts: but still you will see in the

Royal Mile people so queerly cloaked, hatted or shambling that they might have clambered direct from John Knox's Edinburgh, and down below the Castle, where the Grassmarket Mission stands, you may encounter any evening the immemorial figures of Scottish poverty, thick in beards and fustian overcoats, clutching forlorn newspaper-wrapped parcels, but at least smelling warmly of hard liquor, and sometimes bulging reassuringly with bottles.

Here come the Scottish businessmen, bright-eyed but tight-lipped, on their way to the Inland Revenue Department. Here come the Scottish housewives, sweet-smiled but predatory. Here come the ambassadors of the Scottish diaspora, enthusiastically costumed in check bonnets, thistle ties, or even, precariously, kilts, tumbling out of their tourist coaches with cameras at the ready and free introductory samples of Your Own Family Tartan under their arms. The shops are full of Scottish exotica like sporrans or pipe manuals. The skyline is heady with Scottish shapes, brooding tenement houses, crooked chimneys, fretted spires, or the queer crown-cupola of the High Kirk of St. Giles, as telling an emblem of Scottish continuity as the thistle itself.

And in the heart of the Old Town resides that most powerful embodiment of the Scottish idea, the Law. Here in the old Parliament House sits the Court of Session, the High Court of Scotland, its ennobled judges (Lord Keith, Lord Robertson), handing down a law which is one of the oldest and most consistent in the western world, different in kind as in manner from the laws of England, Continental Europe or America. Immovably entrenched within the Royal Mile, the Law carries within itself, century to century, the seed of Scottishness, like a trust. The Scottish monarchy is gone; the Scottish Parliament is gone; the Scottish regiments are absorbed into the British Army; but the Law of Scotland remains inviolate and unique.

'There is a gentleman inside', said the policeman at the door when I sought admission to the Court of Session, 'on trial for murder': so I chose for myself a lesser court, and watched the dignity of Scottish justice dealing with offences less dreadful, like false pretences, driving dangerously or threatening to blow up the Inland Revenue Offices. Any Scottish court is worth visiting, and it is like no other. With its baffling mixture of the formal and the casual, the lofty and the easy-going, it suggests to me less a court of law than a convention of some Highland clan, presided over by its tribal chief and attended by all ranks, laird to crofter.

The Chief here was of course the judge, and undeniably chiefly he looked, crouched over his paper at his high dais, and wearing his tight-curled wig as though it had sprouted spontaneously from his pate in childhood: big-nosed, wrinkle-eyed, high-cheeked, hooded, with eyes that never seemed to blink, and a mouth that expressed, whatever interrogation he supervised, whatever sentence he was decreeing, no flicker of concern, distaste or even particular interest. I could seldom hear what he said, for he spoke in a cracked and high-pitched drone apparently outside my aural range: but I observed that, like an owl peering down from a telegraph wire, he missed no nuance or allusion of the proceedings before him.

One might suppose that with so daunting a mandarin upon the bench, the court below would be subdued. Not at all. It seemed to me a remarkably uninhibited, even a slovenly court. The Clerk was a girl in a blue summer dress, severe in retort but rather sporting in aspect. The usher was a jolly man in a racy zigzag tie. The police sergeant often lost his place charmingly among his papers. The solicitors mostly seemed disconcertingly young, and were often bearded like the tramps of Grassmarket, and looked a little grubby too, I thought, like the tramps again, as though their shoes needed a polish. The lady who sat beside me kept up a steady flow of ribald comment which, though mildly amusing to everyone around us, was, thanks to the density of its Midlothian brogue, inexplicable to me.

Even the accused did not generally seem too depressed, still less browbeaten. This was not, like an English court, the power of crown and state bearing down upon a sinful citizen. It was more like a trial by peers: an assembly of Scotsmen, presided over by a Scottish noble-man, passing judgement upon one of their own number—inheritors all of a common tradition, citizens of a single clan, sinners every one in this degree or that, and familiar every one, I have no doubt, with Rabbie Burns's dictum about 'a man for a' that'.

When I left the court I turned at the door for one last fascinated look at the sheriff, and discovered that, though his slumped posture had apparently not budged an inch, those pale blue eyes of his were staring fixed and motionless into mine—rather as though, like the owl, he could rotate his head without reference to his body, preparatory to dismembering a mouse.

*   *   *

The genius of Edinburgh is essentially harsh or gaunt. The city has produced many men of philosophy, medicine, architecture, art and legal learning, and properly earned for itself in its eighteenth- and early nineteenth-century renaissance the title of Athens of the North. But it is not the humanities that dominate the atmosphere of Auld Reekie: it is more the *in*humanities.

Scotland was always a soldier's country, and the castle that dominates its capital is a soldier's stronghold still. Kilted soldiers, conceited as turkey-cocks in their white spats and ribboned bonnets, stand about its entrance gate with that combination of the virile, the self-conscious and the slightly touching that is unique to the Scottish fighting man. Heroic names abound on notice and memorial, the Royal Scots, the Scots Guards, the Scots Greys, the Black Watch, the Cameron Highlanders. At one o'clock each day a retired Regimental Sergeant Major supervises the ritual firing of the 25-pounder upon the ramparts, coinciding with the drop of a black ball from Nelson's Monument on the other side of the city. ('Nobody can shoot like a Scot', as an old Edinburgh anecdote comments.) And in the huge and infinitely melancholy Scottish National War Memorial, in the heart of the old fortress, are inscribed in book and plaque the names of all those thousands of Scotsmen, from croft and castle, western isle or Glasgow slum, who died in the obscure and terrible sacrifices of the First World War—wandered through even now, every moment of every day, by Scottish folk looking sadly among the registers for the name of Grandad or Uncle Bob.

Evil memories, too, give a cruel frisson to the place. This was the home of Burke and Hare, those virtuoso body-snatchers, whose darkest feats were accomplished within the confines of the Old Town, and whose customer was a dedicated surgeon of the city. At the stake on the Esplanade generations of Scottish witches were burnt or strangled, and in Grassmarket hundreds of Scottish Covenanters, those martyrs to the old faith, were executed for their convictions. From the balcony of Moray House Lady Lorne, on her wedding morning, spat at the doomed Marquis of Montrose, her husband's arch-enemy, as he passed down the street on the way to his execution: in the kitchen of Queensberry House, we are told, in 1700, the insane heir to the Duke of Queensberry murdered a kitchen boy and roasted him upon a spit. The heart-shaped pattern of stones outside St. Giles commemorates not only the legendary Heart of Midlothian, which Scott celebrated, but also the former site of a prison so horrible that to this day traditionalist citizens still spit upon it as they pass—within clear sight of the policemen outside the law courts, for they are given official licence to do so, in a city that is nowadays cleaner than most, but longer of memory too.

All the horrors of medieval kingship, fact or myth, haunt the two royal residences of Edinburgh, the spacious Holyroodhouse at the east end of the Royal Mile, the old royal chambers within the castle at the west. Every room of these fateful households seems to be haunted by tragic ghosts. Here is the room where Bonnie Prince Charlie danced, before leaving for his ignominy at Culloden, and here is the room where Mary Queen of Scots gave birth to the last of the Scottish kings, James VI—a prison-like chamber already, low and narrow, from whose window an immense cliff falls sheer and precipitous from the castle's commanding height to the jumbled thoroughfares below. Uneasy lies the head that wears any crown, but nowhere I think can the cares of monarchy have been more nightmarish than in Auld Reekie long ago.

Killings, necromancy, treachery, exhumations—all these are the very stuff of Edinburgh, and impregnate the city's character. It would be fanciful to suggest that Edinburgh people are much oppressed by so macabre a heritage. On the contrary, for several generations they have most skilfully exploited it, and made the brooding presence of the Old Town one of the great tourist destinations of Europe—even the Edinburgh Festival honours the traditions of war with a searchlight tattoo on the castle esplanade. All the same, these are clearly not citizens of any frivolous provincial resort. Whether they are window-shopping in the New Town or proceeding to a delict or pipe lesson in the Old, they seem to carry the burden of centuries upon their shoulders. They move in a deliberate, stumpy way, as though history is urging them on through fields of mud, and their faces are habitually clamped in introspection. I know of few cities in the world where, walking merrily down a main thoroughfare early on a sunny morning eating an apple, I meet with less vibrant responses: and one is wise to think hard and analytically, before committing oneself to a joke in Edinburgh.

This is not grumpiness exactly, for a few moments with an Edinburgh man soon thaws him, and even reveals a raspy kind of humour. It is the backlog of the past. It is the hard northern climate. It is the sober authority of the Kirk, the bare hills all around, the names in the war memorial, the granite beneath one's feet. It is the wail of pipes and the lowering of flags, it is Mary Queen of Scots, it is the poverty of the ancestral croft, it is the blue eyes of that judge upon his dais, it is cobble-stones, it is haggis, it is Edinburgh.

*   *   *

Edinburgh is a city of tremendous prospects—almost in the heart of the capital rises the mountain called Arthur's Seat, from whose summit on a fine day, as from most such tourist summits the world over, one may see eight counties, ten States, and on a fine day Mount Ararat. The most compelling of the civic views, though, is the one from Calton Hill, a relatively modest eminence that rises immediately beyond the east end of Princes Street, Edinburgh's main shopping street. This is queerly studded with monuments: a domed observatory, the pillars of an uncompleted Parthenon, the memorial to Lord Nelson, shaped like an upturned telescope, from whose summit that black ball drops to the sound of the castle gun, and at whose downstairs window one may sometimes see the curator's wife doing her washing-up, like a figure of Scottish fairy-tale—'What an amazing place to live,' I remarked to her one morning, but 'Ay,' she dispassionately responded, 'it is tha'.'

From here one looks directly down the canyon that separates the plateau of the New Town from the hump-back of the Old. Once it was the loch the developers drained. Now it is partly a garden, and partly a mass of railway tracks, and it provides a dramatic centre-line to the scene. On one side lies the New Town, ordered and geometric, gently running down its slope to the distant blue of the Forth. On the other abruptly rises the castle ridge, like a protrusion from another world, reached by bridges and causeways across the chasm. You might think that the two entities, each superlative in its kind, might strike an even balance, each holding its own against the personality of the other, but it is not so. Auld Reekie wins every time. The New Town looks pallid beside it, overawed despite itself, like some able and imaginative young executive, fresh from management training, outfaced by a criminal self-made tycoon.

And sure enough, though the New Town has made little impact on the Old, on the northern side of the dividing line, incongruous on the edge of the City Fathers' elegant design, a few more profoundly Edinburgh monuments encroach—the black elaborate steeple of the Scott Monument, the three gloomy spires of the Episcopal Cathedral, the ominous thick tower of the North British Hotel. They stand there, on the wrong side of the tracks, like scouts or outposts of Auld Reekie, thinking awful Scottish thoughts, or plotting the downfall of reason.

A PROFITABLE EXILE

On 1 May 1769, Mr. William Hickey, a fashionable, dissolute and engaging young layabout from London, poked his head through the deck-hatch of the East Indiaman *Plassey* (Captain Waddell) for his first sight of India. They had been six months on the voyage from England, sailing via the Cape of Good Hope and the Mozambique Channel, and putting in for provisions in the Comoro Islands north-west of Madagascar. Mr. Hickey was to join the armed forces of the British East India Company, and he carried letters of recommendation to influential men out there, and several very smart uniforms, and a beautiful sword which an old family friend had given him, 'desiring me to cut off half a dozen rich fellows' heads with it'. He had passed his military entrance examination, which consisted of five unmilitary questions, and during the long voyage had drunk a great deal, attended a duel, made an equal number of bosom friends and vehement enemies, and nearly been drowned when his boat capsized in the Comoros.

So on the first day of May he climbed the companion ladder and put his head above deck to see the Coromandel coast. The moment he emerged something terrible happened to him. 'I felt an indescribably unpleasant sensation, suddenly, as it were, losing the power of breathing, which alarmed me much. . . . I could compare it only to standing within the oppressive influence of the steam of a furnace.'

So dreadfully did it strike the young Londoner, so inconceivable did it seem that tolerable human life could be conducted in such an inferno, that almost as soon as he landed young Mr. Hickey was looking around for a passage home again: but it was in fact only the ordinary morning heat of an Indian May, blowing out to sea from the sweltering flatlands of the Carnatic, and in it Hickey was destined to spend the best and most profitable years of his life. 'Cut off half a dozen rich fellows' heads', that old family friend had said, 'and so retire a nabob yourself': and ghastly though that initiation seemed, it was the first essential step in a classic process of eighteenth-century English travel, the making of a nabob.

* * *

By the later years of the eighteenth century India played an inescapable role in the affairs of Great Britain. The British did not rule the subcontinent: they merely possessed a series of settlements along its coast, originally no more than trading posts, by now pseudo-colonies, ostensibly still subject to the potentates of the country, in effect governed, policed and defended by the Honourable East India Company, incorporated by royal charter nearly two centuries before. Though first established by commercial diplomacy, these footholds had been maintained and enlarged by force of arms, and by the 1770s the British were one of several Powers coexisting within India. The French, Dutch and Portuguese settlements were no longer serious rivals, but several great indigenous Powers survived—the Mahratta Confederacy, the Nawab of the Carnatic, the Nizam of Hyderabad and the Sultan of Mysore, the distant Sikhs and Rajputs of the north, and the Mogul Emperor himself, in his fortress-palace at Delhi, who still considered himself suzerain to them all.

The British were the most dynamic of these forces. Though they were endemically at war with the French and the Dutch, they were gradually building up the strength, the knowledge and the system which would eventually make them paramount throughout India. Their territories in the subcontinent were divided into three Presidencies—Madras, Bombay and Bengal—and only in the hinterland of the three seaports did the Company flag fly. Even there its authority was precarious. As recently as 1756 the Nawab of Bengal, reasserting his ancestral rights, had seized Calcutta and suffocated a sizeable proportion of the British population in the Black Hole. The Mahratta chieftains repeatedly threatened Bombay, Madras was intermittently harassed by the Nawabs of the Carnatic. But since 1764, when the Nawab of Bengal had been humiliated once and for all at the battle of Buxar, it had been apparent to seers that the British were in India to stay, not just as traders, but as rulers.

In England the effect of the Indian experience was pervasive rather than dramatic. Only a small minority of Englishmen was concerned with the eastern adventure, and the American colonies and the West Indian sugar islands probably meant more to the general public. But India contributed handsomely to the national wealth, by trading

profits, by the flow of specie, and by loot from the innumerable small
wars fought by the Company's armies in the interests of commerce.
The Company's headquarters in the City of London were unpreten-
tious, but they already contained an unrivalled library of Indian
material, and an Oriental Repository of Indian crafts and objects which
was the nucleus of a great collection. There were Indian warehouses
in several parts of the City, the docks at Blackwall were always
forested with the masts of the Indiamen, and the nabob home from the
east was a familiar figure in English society. Often he made his fortune
in ten or twenty years, and had come home to enjoy it still a young
man, though pale and ravaged by the climate, and often debilitated by
the drink. He frequently brought Indian servants home to cherish him
through his retirement, and he generally bought or built a grand
country house, which he packed with exotic souvenirs, or embellished
in the Hindu style. He was the equivalent of the South African million-
aire a century later: and like the Randlords of a later generation, he
and his kind constituted a forceful political lobby, not merely for old
times' sake, but also because as likely as not he retained business
interests in India, and planned to establish upon them the fortunes of
his family for generations to come.

For India represented opportunity—a national gamble, always there
to be taken up by the spirited, the misfitted or the unwanted. It is true
that in 1773 the British Government, embarrassed by unchecked
excesses of the Company in the past decade, took steps towards its
official control: Warren Hastings was sent out as a royal Governor-
General, frankly representing British sovereignty in India, a Supreme
Court was established to keep some check upon the peculations of the
nabobs, and Parliament at Westminster was given rights of supervision
over the Company's activities. But immense fortunes were still to be
made in India, while the going was good: by merchants and financiers,
by soldiers in pursuit of booty, by professional men of all vocations
ready to exploit the impact of western skills and forms upon the alien
societies of the east. India still offered the chance of getting very rich
exceedingly quick.

So each year the Indiamen assembled magnificently in the English
Channel for the long voyage east, their hulls deep in the water with
merchandise, their protective frigates in attendance, the boatmen from
Dover and Deal bustling around them with messages, or mail, or last-
minute passengers. Every ship carried its quota of young men em-
barking upon their life's adventure in India. Some were respectable

sober-sides. A few were men of scholarly instinct. Many more were adventurers, opportunists, drifters, younger sons, people without a purpose, nuisances perhaps, packed off with relief by exhausted parents, or having a go at India *faute de mieux*, without any particular avocation in mind. One such young man was William Hickey who, though he looked very splendid, he thought, in his uniforms, nevertheless had no very serious intention of adopting the military life, and had indeed no idea at all of what he wanted to do, beyond pursuing, as he had done with mixed success for the twenty years of his life so far, a career of uninterrupted carnal satisfaction.

* * *

We would know little of Hickey if there had not been published between 1913 and 1925 four volumes of his memoirs, meticulously recorded in his later years in a huge vellum-bound volume, and running to well over half a million words. As it is, we know him very well. He was a familiar English type then, as he is now. 'A slip slop, moll dawdling boy', is how a half-drunk sea-captain at Deal described him, tempting him to drive up to London for an evening's pleasure before sailing to India next day. 'Damn me if ever I saw such milk sop poor devils as ye are. What's got into the present race! There is not an ounce of proper spirit about them . . . you wishy-washy soft masters, fresh from mammy's apron-strings, have no nounce. Damn me, there's nothing in ye; no, nothing in ye.'

The captain knew better really, and so do we. Of course Hickey got horses at once, and drove to London through the night for a frenzied few hours of self-indulgence. He was a wastrel in his teens, certainly, less than absolutely honest, loose-living, heedless: but he was no slip slop dawdling boy. He was only waiting his time. The son of a well-respected London lawyer, educated at Westminster, he was one of those young men of the upper middle classes whose fate it is to gravitate to grander circumstances, getting themselves as a result constantly into debts and deceit. Mr. Hickey senior was not at all a severe father, and in his way Mr. Hickey junior much loved him: but time and again the son let the father down, running away from his tutor's to sleep with a whore in Drury Lane, piling up debts, spending other people's money. He worked for a time in his father's office, and thus gained, more by useful connections than by diligence, legal qualifications: but all his energies went in pleasure, the pleasures of the tavern, the recreation garden, unexpectedly the river (for he loved

rowing and sailing), predictably the brothel. His stamina was tremendous, his high spirits were marvellously infectious. Women loved him,
as he loved them all his life, and his friends were mostly picaresques
of his own kind: spendthrift younger sons, wild Guards officers, rakes
and roués of every background.

He had a wonderful time of it, between calamities. After repeated
disillusionments his father barred him from the family home, but he
relented in the end, as everyone knew he would: for young Mr.
Hickey, though certainly adept at the sowing of wild oats, was really
a very nice boy underneath—soft-hearted, quick to remorse, generous,
always kind to his inferiors, and even in his worst misbehaviours of
the small hours, really no more than a bit of a lad. India was just the
place for him: and though his first attempt, as a military cadet, was an
abject failure, in 1777 he made a second start, as a lawyer in Calcutta.
This time he found his niche. He was a success. 'Although my follies',
says he in his memoirs, '(not to use a harsher term) were so numerous
and so often repeated, yet my honoured father lived long enough to
see an end of them, and most heartily and affectionately to congratulate me upon my having at last steadily settled in a fair, industrious
and honourable line of life, universally esteemed and respected in the
society amongst whom I resided. Thank God that such has been the case!'

*   *   *

By then Calcutta, the largest, richest and gayest of the British
settlements in India, was a city of incipient splendour. It had been
founded a century before on the banks of the Hooghly, one of the
mouths of the Ganges, and was fast becoming the focal point of north-
east India, a magnet for the trade and wealth of all Bengal. Its name
honoured the goddess Kali, most bloodthirsty of the Hindu pantheon,
but the British had given it the epithet City of Palaces. It was like an
eighteenth-century Brasilia. Its form was not yet moulded, its gaps
were not filled in, the trees had not grown, the parks were not green
yet, and it had the bare scoured look of new towns everywhere, before
time matures and muddles them.

Architecturally its style was neo-classical, which had, with its
suggestions of past imperial splendours, symbolic meanings for the
British overseas. Its showpiece was the Esplanade, a row of public
buildings running at right angles to the river, and designed to make a
grandiose impression upon the newcomer arriving from the sea (an
impression only belied, for those travellers curious enough to explore,

by the jumble of hovels which were already arising to house the growing Indian population behind). There was a court house, a Council House, the Accountant-General's office, Government House. Not far away was the Writers' Building, the administrative office of the Company, and there was a new steepled church, St. John's, which bore a comforting resemblance to St. Martin-in-the-Fields at home. Fort William, the principal British stronghold in Bengal, was surrounded by a wide open space, the Maidan, which was created to provide a clear field of fire for the garrison, but which also made a magnificent park: and all along the river banks, from Garden Reach downstream far up towards Barrackpore in the north, the rich Britons of Calcutta had erected their homes on a lavish scale—porticoed and pillared mansions, their shutters generally painted a vivid green, covered in white stucco, surrounded by large compounds and cluttered servants' quarters, and built in the manner of very imposing Palladian country houses at home.

It seemed at first sight a proper European city, resplendently white—for nearly every building was new, and expensive. Yet to percipient visitors it presently came to feel curiously insubstantial. Those splendid Grecian façades were generally only made of brick, stuccoed over, and soon began to peel and crumble. The Palladian style was meant to be interpreted in the most durable of materials, and its reproduction in Bengal, where its splendours were plaster-thin and often jerry-built, thus possessed a quality of sad parody. Those mansions were like exhibition buildings, not meant to last: and this was true in a sense, for though many of them have survived to this day, the Englishmen who built them had no intention of inhabiting them for long, but wished only to make their fortunes and be off. Little sense of duty, mission or even stability yet informed the British presence in Bengal. It was there to make money, and make money it did.

This was Hickey's intention too. His second start in India was made when he was twenty-nine, older then than it sounds now, and he must have felt that this time it was all or nothing. In such a frame of mind, no doubt, countless Englishmen had disembarked at Garden Reach before him, and thousands more would do so during the next 150 years—for to the very end of the British Empire there was a certain desperation to the moment when, disembarking amid the stinks, the hubbub and the indescribable heat of India, one realized that this was to be, for the best part of a lifetime, home. (Why did the sahibs ever go to India, a fastidious Maharajah once asked Lord Curzon, when they could stay at home on their English lawns playing flutes and watching the rabbits?)

Hickey soon made himself known to all the right people, and thanks more to his father's reputation than his own, was promptly admitted Solicitor, Attorney and Proctor of the new Supreme Court. Later he set up house with an English mistress, Charlotte Barry, who was indulgently recognized by the predominantly masculine community as his wife, and her presence at the Calcutta ceremony called 'setting up' set the seal upon Hickey's entry into Bengal society: for seated in a chair at the head of their drawing-room, with ladies in attendance on either side, for three successive evenings she received all the females of the settlement, each escorted by at least two gentlemen, with curtseys, polite salutations and awkward silences, from seven in the evening till after eleven—a preposterous ritual, Hickey thought it, and soon to become obsolete, as the handful of nabobs in eighteenth-century Calcutta gave way to the Victorian multitude of officials and box-wallahs.

Charlotte, poor soul, could not stand the climate, and died after only six months in Bengal: but Hickey himself, solaced in later years by Indian mistresses, lived a life of developing luxury and distinction, often ill but always resilient, surviving the worst the monsoons could do to him, growing perceptibly more temperate as the years went by, busy from dawn till dusk in a rewarding round of litigation, social effervescence, private feud, ostentation, gourmandizing or inebriation. There were, of course, Englishmen of more serious bent in Calcutta, artists, linguists, historians, cultured men like Hastings himself, who lived in Government House in stoic abstinence, interested himself in everything from Hindu philosophy to Himalayan botany, and was deeply concerned with the purpose and method of the British presence in India. Hickey though, we may suppose, was in many ways a fairly characteristic Anglo-Indian gentleman of Bengal, and in his diaries he recorded just what such a destiny entailed, in the last years of the nabobs (for by the end of his career in India, their days were clearly numbered).

*   *   *

It entailed the possibility of danger, for the turn of the century was full of risks in India. The Black Hole was fresh in everyone's memories, and the city was still fortified against attack from the interior. The British hold on Bengal was by no means impregnable, and rioting in the city was not uncommon. Besides, England remained at war with France, and there were times when Admiral de Suffren's squadron, aggressively cruising about the Indian Ocean, seemed quite likely to fall upon Bengal. The Hickeys themselves were temporarily de Suffren's prisoners, during a voyage from England in 1783, and not until Trafalgar was the French threat entirely removed. Like British merchants in Hong Kong today, the nabobs of Calcutta knew always at the backs of their minds that only a relatively small change in the fortunes of the world would mean their utter and irrevocable ruin.

Then the health hazard was appalling. Two monsoons, it was popularly said, was the life of the Briton in Calcutta, and Hickey's memoirs are full of ghastly diseases and scarcely less ghastly treatments. Cholera was worst of all. Nobody knew what caused it: some thought eating fish and meat at the same meal incited it, others believed it hovered unpredictably over the city in vaporous clouds: one method of treatment was the application of a red-hot iron ring to the patient's navel, a course of action which would, experts convincingly claimed, cause 'a sudden revolution in the intestines'. Typhoid and malaria, both mysteries to medical science, were endemic in Bengal: unnamed fevers carried people off with fearful suddenness. One of the most impressive corners of the infant city was the cemetery in South Park Street, opened in 1763 and a town of its own already, laid out in streets and forums of classical pavilions, taken direct from the textbooks of Palladian architecture, beneath whose correctly proportioned domes and pyramids the English of the City of Palaces were palatially interred —most of them young, most of them hopeful, all sacrificed *au fond* to the pursuits of profit.

Just the climate itself was hazard enough. Though by the end of the century ice could be bought at the Ice House (it came from Wenham Lake in Massachusetts) most families had to make do with an earthen-ware jar kept cool by a servant whose sole duty it was to rotate it in a tank of water and saltpetre. The middle of every day was a nightmare for the overdressed and overfed English, and then the community went to sleep behind its green shutters, while the punkahs creaked above their heads, swayed by invisible serfs, and the blessed shadows crept across the city from the west. Everything had to be done in the five or six cooler hours of the day—before breakfast, when they took their exercise, and even held their race meetings, in the forenoon when they worked in the offices, late in the evening when they trooped to the New Playhouse or the Harmonic Tavern, in the small hours when, after an enormous dinner, they proceeded to dance till dawn—women often died, we are told, from the strain of Calcutta's all-night dances.

It was not, for all its festivity, an easy life. 'Oh damn the place,' said one of Hickey's Bengal friends, when asked in London if he were missing Calcutta, 'don't mention it. I should be devilish glad never to be obliged to see it again so long as I live.' Yet by and large, it seems, that little expatriate society of Britons, deposited in their lace and spangles upon the Hooghly's humid banks, lived out their exiles not merely with resignation or resolution, but actually with gusto.

*   *   *

The city was full of characters. Warren Hastings himself was one of the most remarkable Britons ever to serve in India, and was later to provide the epilogue to the whole gaudy drama of nabobdom: his impeachment in 1788 for misconduct in India, though six years later he was acquitted of all charges, was really a reminder from England that, however powerful and princely Englishmen might seem in Bengal, by metropolitan standards they were still ordinary citizens of the Crown—a reminder, in fact, of reality to a community that liked to live in fantasy. Then there was the impetuous and malignant Philip Francis, who fought a duel with Hastings and was one of Hickey's particular *bêtes noires*, and Sir Elijah Impey, the haughty Chief Justice, and Hickey's close friend Bob Pott, whom he first met as a seaman cadet in Canton, and who was already, in his twenties, a well-known Calcutta character. The Begum Johnson survived four husbands to keep open house every night of the year and become grandmother to a Prime Minister, Lord Liverpool; Miss Emma Wrangham was a splendid shot and a formidable boxer; the Reverend Mr. Blunt had habits unbecoming to a clergyman—an incomprehensible young man, Hickey calls him, who got 'abominably drunk and in that disgraceful condition exposed himself to both soldiers and sailors, running out stark naked into the midst of them, talking all sorts of bawdy and ribaldry.'

Even in the racy and not very scrupulous England of George III, not all these people would have been welcome in fastidious society at home—'Take care of the spoons and forks,' another Calcutta character, Colonel Auchmuty, used to say to his wife before the guests arrived, 'count them up carefully, my honey, for by the holy Jesus we have got some tight boys here tonight.' The nabobs lived with wild extravagance. It is true that their palaces were often half furnished, and that a certain air of unreality attended the very existence of British Bengal, but the pace of life was terrific. Mrs. Mary Sherwood, the children's writer, called it 'splendid' sloth and languid debauchery', but though there was a certain splendour to the heedlessness of Calcutta life, there seems very little languor to the debauchery. They gambled madly: it was not unknown to lose £40,000 in an evening. They drank enormously: three bottles of claret in an evening was normal for a man, and most women of style got through a bottle a night. They ate gargantuan meals of mutton, curries, cheeses and fruits, and entertained themselves at the dinner table with a game fashionable in Calcutta then, the flicking of bread pellets across the room.

They had coveys of servants, and drove about in smart crested phaetons, or rode through the Maidan on exquisite Arabs. Hickey himself indulged his life-long penchant for boats by building himself a ceremonial barge, rowed by a crew of fourteen in red, green and white liveries, and in this handsome craft he would row his guests up and down the Hooghly in the evening, attended sometimes by small pages in turbans, blowing French horns through the dusk. Bachelors nearly all had mistresses, generally Indians, or half-castes, though Francis kept a gorgeous Frenchwoman in a country house up-river, and Hickey's own Charlotte had been an expensive *demi-mondaine* in London.

But behind the vulgarity, the ostentation and the hedonism, a more serious purpose lay. Most of these people did not want to stay in Calcutta a year longer than they must. They lived lavishly indeed, but as a means of escape: for no nabob in his senses wished to retire in Bengal, and no nabob at all expected to return to England without a sizeable fortune to his credit—though as it happened many of them, so imprudently did they live, went home penniless and forlorn.

* * *

As a lawyer Hickey made his money largely by representing rich Indians in the European courts, where English was the official language. Almost as soon as he set up practice in Calcutta he found he had clients, and for the next twenty-five years he was never short of income (though often, being the kind of man he was, distinctly short of capital—setting up an establishment for Charlotte, complete with a good cellar of wines, a London-built carriage and her own hairdresser brought out from London, kept him in debt at 12 per cent for more than twenty years).

Straight vocational earnings, though, provided only a small part of

India's opportunities. Every kind of supplementary corruption thrived, and vast sums of money poured into British purses almost effortlessly. Generals could make their fortunes by a single battle, and senior company men, or civic dignitaries of Calcutta, could do almost as well. Hastings himself once contemplated bringing recalcitrant members of his Council to heel by a general measure of bribery—£10,000 apiece would do the trick, he thought. Most lucrative of all were posts as British residents at the courts of Indian princes, for they controlled access not only from the public to the prince, but from the prince to his effectual suzerains, the British. One British official, at the court of the Nawab of the Carnatic, is said to have picked up £1,200,000 in bribes in nineteen years. Hickey's friend Bob Potts became resident at the Durbar of the Nawab of Bengal (by pulling strings in London and bribing his predecessor to retire). There he found that the entire stipend paid to the Nawab by the British passed through his own hands, 'in which channel a considerable part of it always stuck to his fingers', and he also enjoyed the 'further advantage' of supervising all the Nawab's purchases of European articles. The Resident at Benares, another friend of Hickey's, was reckoned to make some £30,000 a year in bribes: he had got the job through the influence of his father, the Archbishop of York.

*   *   *

By the time Mr. Hickey went home for good, in 1808, his Calcutta was already disappearing, and his kind of Briton, too, was fading from the Indian scene. Graver men of sterner duty were arriving to administer the Indian Empire, and authority was passing by stages out of the hands of a trading monopoly into the care of an imperial government. Bread-flicking was out. The formidable Wellesley turned Calcutta into a great capital by building for himself and his successors a truly imperial palace—India, it was said, should be ruled 'with the ideas of a Prince, not with those of a retail-dealer in muslins'. One by one the old perquisites of graft or privilege were abolished, until in the end the last traces of the whole archaic structure were swept away by the Indian Mutiny. The nabobs were figures of the eighteenth century, and so with their foibles and their vices, their jollity, their crooked fortunes, their ravaged livers and their sallow complexions, their little Indian servants, their ivory gee-gaws and their interminable tales of life in Bengal, they retreated before the nineteenth century and went home to die.

Hickey himself went with regret, for despite that appalling first glimpse of the Indian coast, he grew to love Bengal, and became one of the best-known personalities of British India, prominent at every party, every ball, every race-meeting, promenading through the Maidan in his elegant phaetons or rowed so flamboyantly among the country craft and three-masters on the river. By the time he retired, in his sixtieth year, he was the master of a household of sixty-three servants, and he took home a fortune of some £19,000—not a large one by the standard of the nabobs, but then he was never the kind to save. He acquired a pleasant small house at Beaconsfield in Buckinghamshire, and there he settled with his two maiden sisters and his Indian servant Munnoo, and wrote his memoirs: for he had experienced the truth, he tells us, of an observation he had frequently heard— 'viz, that want of employment is one of the greatest miseries that can be attached to a mind not altogether inactive.'

ANGLO-CHINA

A foreign devil of my acquaintance, on my first morning in Hong Kong, took me to the top of an exceedingly high mountain, by funicular from Garden Road, and invited me to worship.

The kingdoms of the world lay before us. The skyscrapers of Victoria, jam-packed at the foot of the hill, seemed to vibrate with pride, greed, energy and success, and all among them the traffic swirled, and the crowds milled, and the shops glittered, and the money rang. Beyond lay the ships in their hundreds, like a vast fleet anchored in the roadsteads from Chai Wan to Stonecutter's Island, here a super-tanker, here a cruise ship, there a warship all a'bristle, with their attendant sampans busy beside them, and the junks and tugs and pilot boats hurrying everywhere, and the hydrofoil foaming off to Macao, and the ceaseless passage of the Star ferries backwards and forwards across the harbour. Across the water lay Kowloon on the mainland: deep among its structures ran the great gash of Nathan Road, violent with advertising, and off to the east the airport protruded brutally into the harbour, and sometimes a jet threw itself screaming and smoking into the sky.

Beyond it all again lay the hills of China, but these my guide ignored. His eyes were focussed, intense, almost fanatical, upon that brilliant pulsation at our feet, moving from ship to bank building, harbour-front to hotel, like the most diligent of landowners surveying his inherited estate. 'You may not like it,' he said. 'We don't ask you to like it. We don't *expect* you to like it. But you must admit it *works*.'

* * *

He meant that it worked in a Victorian, ideological sense, like a steam-pump as an agency of Progress, or some unarguable theory of the Manchester School. It is certainly true that Hong Kong has a greased, thumping feel to it, suggestive of well-turned brass pistons, or persuasive statistics. In the reference books, or on the map, it seems a weird political and economic anomaly: on the spot it feels, if not exactly organic, at least habitual. It has been there a long time. There is a mystic saying in Hong Kong that one must not express an opinion about the place until one has been there for nineteen years: but the corporate experience of the place has now lasted for four or five generations, since that fateful 26 January 1841, when the Royal Navy raised the flag on the foreshore at Possession Point—just along the road, that is, from the Macao hydrofoil station. 'There can be neither safety nor honour for either the British or the Chinese', Captain Charles Elliot, R.N., had declared, 'until Her Majesty's flag flies on these coasts in a secure position': and since then no British Government, and perhaps no Chinese either, has seriously considered lowering the Union Jack again, and returning Hong Kong to its hinterland.

It may look precarious in *The Statesman's Year Book*, but it is an

Oriental fact of life. Poised minutely, all 400 square miles of it, upon the skin of China, it is a sort of permanent parasite. It is divided into two constitutional parts. Hong Kong Island, with the mainland peninsula of Kowloon, is British by right of possession, ceded in perpetuity by the Chinese: the New Territories, 365 square miles of the adjacent mainland, are British by virtue of a ninety-nine-year lease, expiring in 1998. But though to outsiders there sounds a crucial difference between these two categories, the one organically British, the other British by licence, so to speak, when you are there they both seem much the same. The present Chinese Government, as it happens, does not recognize the New Territories lease anyway, so that the date of its expiry is more than usually hypothetical even by diplomatic standards, and the British would probably put it out of their minds were it not for the fact that land tenure in the Territories is inevitably linked with the expiry date, so that a reminder of 1998 appears on every deed of estate. No frontier divides the one part from the other, and though to gentlemen abed in England there may seem something risky to an investment that theoretically collapses in twenty-five years, capitalists in Hong Kong seldom seem to give the matter a thought, and behave as though the whole place will be true-blue British for ever.

And if the parasite is well established, it is also full of the life-force—bile, venom, adrenalin, according to your diagnosis. More than four million people live in Hong Kong. Its port handles 7,000 ocean-going ships a year. It is a great producer of textiles, toys, plastics, electronics, and one of the most brilliant and bullish of the world's entrepôts. If you consider it as part of the almost vanished British Empire, then it is more populous than all the rest of the Empire put together. If you think of it as part of China, it is the third biggest Chinese city, and easily the richest. On the one hand it is a dazzling showcase of western capitalism, on the other a microcosm of China herself, within whose cramped and isolated confines there live emigrants from every Chinese province, class and philosophy.

It ticks, wriggles and itches there, on the edge of Kwangtung Province—sometimes an irritant to the People's Republic, perhaps, but a safety valve too, and perhaps even a comfort. Whatever else I felt about Hong Kong, when my friend on the Peak invited me to admire it, I did not think it in the least temporary. It is always rash to prophesy political longevity, as Voltaire realized when, waking up in Paradise one day in 1798, he remembered his forecast that the Venetian Republic would last for ever: but this I will take the risk of saying, that like many another anomaly, Hong Kong may well outlive the norm. It reminds me of those quirks of English society, wrinkled customs, immemorial exceptions, which linger on through change and election all the more tenaciously because they stand outside the rules.

'What an anachronism!' people exclaim. 'A British colonial Government, totally unrepresentative, like something out of Victoria's day, lording it over four million Chinese! How do the Chinese stand for it?' They stand for it, I think, largely because they *are* Chinese. They know a useful compromise when they see one, and so well does the device of Hong Kong suit their needs and genius that for all I know they invented the arrangement themselves, like everything else, 10,000 years ago in Soochow.

* * *

The Chineseness of Hong Kong, unlike the tempered Chineseness of Singapore, is so terrific, so furious, so complex in texture that I have always despaired of capturing its sensations in words, and on my first visit to the colony, in 1958, I was reduced to a symbolic description of the clumps of edible frogs, tied together around the waist and still vigorously alive, which are the piquant prodigies of the Central Market. I cannot do much better now. The noise, the push, the sheer physical mass of the Chinese in Hong Kong overwhelms the senses, and reduces the most grandiloquent writer to vignette.

Take, for instance, for a start, one's arrival at one of the second-class hotels with grand names which cluster, gaudy with neon lights, around the waterfront end of Nathan Road. This is a dauntingly Chinese experience. The doorman indeed is probably a turbaned Sikh, offering old imperialists a poignant reminder of better times, but inside the lobby everything is garishly Chinese. Tasteless, loud and faintly suggestive of humdrum varieties of sin, it is nevertheless exceedingly efficient. The receptionist throws you a steely gold-toothed smile, but has your reservation at her finger-tips. The porter's greeting is perfunctory, but you can be sure he has the right key. The room itself is clean, and has plenty of towels, and lots of hot water, and a list of Girlie Clubs prepared for your comfort by the Tourist Association.

But ah, when the porter closes your door, and you are left in that small cubby-hole of Hong Kong, how more than impersonal, how dehumanized the place turns out to be! You look out through the metal-framed windows, and across the great filthy pit of the hotel, littered with old sacks and piles of discarded masonry, a huge slab of building confronts you. All its windows are brilliantly lit, and in each a little Chinese cameo, separate from all its neighbours, is joylessly displayed. Here four girls sit tense over their sewing-machines, silent and unsmiling, motionless but for the quick twist and tug of their fingers. There a solitary shirt-sleeved man is hunched over his files and calculators, beneath the dazzling light of his naked bulb, dead to all else and perhaps to himself. Along the way eight or nine families seem to be packed into one room, and one sees only flashes of infant limbs, waves of drapery, buckets, black loose hair, bedclothes and grinning mop faces, as though some perpetual and appalling farce is being played inside.

Every room is ablaze, every room full, and across the intervening gloom one hears radios, clicking machines, shouts and children's screams. In another city all that life over there might be a comfort, a reminder that if you happen to be alone that night, all around you is the warmth of community. In Hong Kong it is different. Nobody out there seems to take the slightest notice of anyone else—let alone of you as, peering through the orange fabric curtains, your wan western face gazes aghast across the chasm.

* * *

At another Chinese extreme, take the walled village of Kam Tin, which stands antique and morose in the heart of the New Territories. This is Chineseness of a very different sort. It is not a very large walled village, but it is one of the tourist sights of the colony, for better than any other local monument, perhaps, it evokes the continuity of the Chinese presence—antedating as it does by four centuries the arrival of Her Majesty's frigates upon the foreshore. Kam Tin is Chinese in a tortoisean way, a carapacial, scaly way. Modernity has long besieged it, and just across the way there is a garage, and a small supermarket: but the village lies hot and secretive still within its towered walls, and the Teng clan, who built it in the first place, live in it exclusively still. Wrinkled crones in black pyjamas and coolie hats guard it, half-heartedly offering a selection of spurious antiques, and an aged man in black directs you to the slot in the wall in which you are invited to place your charitable offering. Then through the wrought-iron gate you pass, and into the brown brick labyrinth beyond.

It is the very opposite of picturesque. Rectangular, dowdy, brown, it reminded me of old Swindon, down by the locomotive works.

Everybody seems immensely old in Kam Tin. Old dogs lie about. Old ladies look at you through unglazed windows. Old flies buzz. There is no sound of traffic, for no wheeled vehicles can enter, except for a few old bicycles: so a hush hangs over the place, a very old Chinese hush, pursuing you down the narrow alleyways, between the drab mud-brick houses, like a venerable reproach, or a dictum. I found it all rather unnerving, and seemed to feel the oldness of Kam Tin clinging to me when I left, impregnating my clothes and my thoughts, until at last I overpowered it with peeled shrimps and fried rice in the floating restaurant at Sha Tin Hoi.

* * *

But for a last, blither cameo of Hong Kong's Chinadom, let me take you to the small island which stands, linked by a causeway to the shore, on the edge of Tolo Harbour, north of Kowloon. There is a house upon the island, but we will circumvent it, and scramble around the bluff below until we reach the little point at the end, where the grass is prickly and sun bleached, and small bright flowers have gone feral from the garden above. Behind us now we may hear a radio from the kitchen, or children's laughter from an upstairs room, but before us lies classic China. The bay extends blue and limpid towards the China Sea, and beyond it lie low tawny hills, speckled here and there with villages, hot, dusty, arid: and in the still basin below us ten or twelve junks lie, tied close together in twos and threes, like painted ships.

Their awkward but elegant forms, high-prowed, top-heavy, are reflected romantically in the water, and sometimes there are signs of life upon them: men moving ropes about, women emerging with pots or laundry, children scrambling among the rigging. Generally, though, they seem to lie there motionless, as if for show. It is a scene of infinite calm and balance, a posed scene. It is as though those painted vessels never move from their moorings, but lie there for ever as upon a china plate, lovingly etched and baked in the glaze, and traditionally coloured.

* * *

They are not there for artistic reasons. They are there to make money. Making money is the purpose of Hong Kong, and it was the prospect of profit that induced the British to found the colony in the first place. The great British merchants of Hong Kong, the *taipans* who first made their fortunes in opium and tea, have never relaxed their grip upon the opportunities of the place, and have survived war, depression and the end of Empire to remain great men of the China coast. 'Look, there goes the *taipan*,' Chinese people sometimes say, when they see one of the moguls of Jardine Matheson sweep by in his limousine: and though they say it partly in fun (the commonest kind of *taipan* is a chief pimp), and partly by force of habit, they also speak out of an empathetic esteem. The British and the Chinese may spring from utterly alien cultures, from opposite ends of the world, but they are fused in the furnace of Hong Kong, and made colleagues by the hope of profit.

The rich British still live very grandly. They appear with visiting earls in gossip columns, and form a well-known element in the entrepreneurial jet set that swishes about between Beirut, London, New York, Tokyo and Sydney. 'I'm so sorry,' I was told when I inquired after a friend of a friend, 'but Mrs. W— is away in Japan, launching a ship.' They have country houses on the delectable eastern shore of Hong Kong Island, they have closed-circuit colour television in their boxes at Happy Valley race-track, and so long have they been on the China coast, if not in person then at least by the proxy of their forebears, that the quirks of Hong Kong life have become their orthodoxies. Peking holds no mystery for them: they have maintained their contacts with China through the Kuomintang and Cultural Revolution, and they regard the aspirations of Chiang and Chou alike with an urbane indulgence. *Plus ça change*, they seem to shrug, and ringing for a specially bound copy of the company's annual report, with their compliments, they draw your attention to last year's highly satisfactory trading account.

Hong Kong nowadays is only their base, and their activities extend, in shipping and trading, banking and insurance, speculation and agency, all over the Far East. Even so their stake in the colony is staggering. Wherever you look there stand the artefacts and enterprises of Jardine Matheson, Butterfield & Swire, and the other old houses of the British connection: mammoth new office blocks, enormous shopping complexes, a tunnel under the harbour, the China Motor Bus Company, swank hotels, graving docks, television services. They have their fingers in innumerable pies, and they are still distinctly British. When Jardine built their vast new headquarters building, the tallest structure in Asia unless you count television towers, the architects were Palmer & Turner, the consultant engineers were Mitchell McFarlane, the air-conditioning was by Jardine Engineering Company, the tiling was by Marley, and only the hinges, so I discovered from the board at the construction site, were by Shun Fung.

If the Chinese acquire an alarming new bite and dominance when they leave their homeland, so do the overseas British, and British capitalism in Hong Kong retains an edge and confidence it has long lost at home. There is no sentimentality to the *taipans*. They are pushing men in a men's world, and their wives, I am told, sometimes get bored with their perpetual enrichment, handed down from father to son, and pine for more modest indulgences, like a concert now and then, or a visiting poet.

* * *

There are poorer Britons too, of course. You often see them on the Star ferry, open-necked or cotton-frocked, browned by the China sun, and bearing themselves like what they are—almost the last of the workaday British colonialists.

Some are sailors, and are on their way to the China Fleet Club, that almost legendary institution, familiar to a million matelots, which stands on the edge of the Suzy Wong country beside the waterfront of Wanchai. Some are soldiers—stationed in Hong Kong not to keep the Chinese Communists out, but, as official handouts discreetly say, 'to assist the Government in maintaining security and stability', the classic role of British imperial forces. Many more are accountants, clerks, or housewives, who speak in Londonish or more probably Surreyish accents, and tend to grumble about the servant problem. Some are technical advisers, or journalists, or airline pilots, or university teachers. Nearly all are unmistakably British. There are Europeans of many sorts in Hong Kong and more than 6,000 Americans, too: but the British vastly predominate—there are nearly 30,000 of them—and in some indefinable way they remain different from all the others, too, and even now carry themselves apart.

I loved to sit on the ferry and contemplate these people. They were trapped for me there, like historical specimens, deep in their tabloids or compiling their shopping lists. What a line they represented, I used to think! What generations of exiles culminated in their persons, listlessly looking out across the passing harbour, or doing the cross-word puzzle! Their fathers blazed a way across the world, veld to outback, pioneering in shacks, beachcombing on reefs, disciplining recalcitrant Sioux or bayonetting fuzzy-wuzzies: and here they were beside me, the last of the long parade, indifferent to their origins,

unconscious of them perhaps, unexcited on the slat-seated ferry-boat
between Kowloon and Victoria!

The boat shudders; the gangplanks clatter down, top and lower deck;
the blue-jerseyed Chinese seamen swing open the iron gates; in a
trice, as the crowd streams off the vessel and hastens beneath the
subway into town, those unobtrusive imperialists are overwhelmed
by their Chinese fellow subjects, four million to 30,000, and you
would hardly guess from the look of things that there was a Briton
left in the crown colony at all.

* * *

Yet Britons still rule it, directly and absolutely. The Governor and
Commander-in-Chief of Hong Kong is still guarded by Gurkha
sentries in his white palace below the Botanical Gardens, and un-
glamorously installed in rambling Indianified offices, or making do in
temporary shacks, the Hong Kong Government is modestly at work.
Most of its senior members are British, some of them Chinese-speaking,
most of them staunch believers in the rightness of their own methods.
They do not merely rule Hong Kong, indeed; they rule it absolutely.
Subject only to the distant distracted authority of Queen, Parliament
and Whitehall, the Governor and his officials are as all-powerful now
as their colleagues were a century ago in India or Bermuda. No local
legislature restrains them. The only elected representatives in Hong
Kong are members of the Urban Council, and even they are in a
minority, and represent only a minute proportion of the population.
Both the Executive and the Legislative Councils of the Colony are
entirely *ex officio* or nominated by Government, and both are presided
over by the Governor. The Empire lives in Hong Kong. With names
like Luddington, Haddon-Cave or Lightbody, with duck suits and
straw hats, with a formidable expertise and a truly dedicated zeal, the
gentlemen of the Hong Kong administration direct the affairs of the
last of the great crown colonies superbly in the tradition of the later
Raj.

'Hong Kong subscribes', one distinguished public official observed
to me, 'to Victorian economic principles: these are the only economic
principles that have ever actually *succeeded*.' *Taipans* may complain of
too much official interference: officials believe themselves to be oper-
ating the last of the *laissez-faire* administrations. Hong Kong is a free
port; it is charged by the energies of free enterprise; even the great
civic works, the public transport, the harbour tunnel, are financed

largely by private money. Government in Hong Kong is unobtrusive partly because it cannot afford flamboyance, but partly because it believes its function to be supplementary. 'Our job is to do the things private enterprise cannot or will not do, and to keep the whole caboodle on the rails.'

It suggests to me a conscientious vicar in a particularly well-heeled parish, pagan, rather condescending but not by and large unfriendly. Until the 1950s the British Government regarded Hong Kong more or less as any other colony, and schemes were prepared for constitutional reform: today there is no pretence to liberalism, but the colony's officials are essentially philanthropic in their approach. No taint of jingo vulgarizes their attitudes, and they are rightly hurt when visitors suspect them of snobbery or racialism. They are the very opposite of your stock imperialists, and are proud of Hong Kong chiefly as a haven, which has welcomed so many millions of refugees, over many generations, and has done its best to support them fairly. Nor are they in the least chauvinist. It did not seem to me, I innocently observed to one of them, that Hong Kong *felt* British at all—look at the way the traffic moved! 'I agree with you there,' he replied. 'Good road manners are dead in Britain.'

They say that pragmatism was always an imperial quality, and in Hong Kong it is certainly evident. The British rulers of the place have been obliged to live not for the ideal, not even for the principle, but for the situation. Other colonies may have had leisure for introspection, for historical awareness and cultural ambitions; Hong Kong has no museum, a public library smaller than Fiji's, and an archive only established in the past couple of years. Some British colonies were always fortresses; some were settlements; some were transit stations on the imperial routes. Hong Kong was always a place of profit, and when Captain Ellis spoke of safety and honour all those years ago, he was really thinking of capital and dividends. To this overriding purpose the Hong Kong Government has always adapted its attitudes, and very successfully too. It has had few rebels within its ranks, demanding emancipation or self-government; it has recognized itself primarily as a law-and-order government, perpetually holding a ring, and with works of goodwill thrown in as a sideline; and to every criticism it offers, like my friend on the Peak, that last rationalization of imperial pragmatism: '*It works!*'

*　　*　　*

In some ways it is an ugly mechanism. Hong Kong is a very beautiful place, full of colour and of splendour, but it is charmless. It is hard and humourless. It ought to lift the spirits, with its marvellous vistas, its perpetual surge of energy, its contrasts and its anomalies: in fact it somehow falls flat. Hong Kong is generally popularly coupled with Rio, Sydney and San Francisco as one of the loveliest harbour cities in the world: of the four it is the biggest, liveliest and perhaps even the richest, but to my tastes it is also the least invigorating.

I think this is partly because, for reasons I cannot analyse, the confrontation between Chinese and British lacks piquancy, or even style. It is rather an *ordinary* meeting. I went one day to visit an acquaintance in one of the big apartment blocks that have lately been built beside the Kowloon waterfront. These are inhabited almost entirely by Chinese, but they look rather like a corner of Sheffield, say, and offer a peculiarly dispiriting combination of life-styles. Into those moulds of concrete, by Greater London Council out of Radiant City, have been squeezed all the dourest qualities of the Chinese. The buildings are indistinguishable from each other, there seem to be a million more or less identical tenants on every floor, and nobody appears to know anybody else. It is as though they are all in immediate competition with one another, for air or living space, so that the *bonhomie* is removed from Yorkshire, the comradeship from Canton, and one is left with a formidable but unlovely hybrid.

Formidable, because there is no breath of the haphazard to this life-style: the Hong Kong Chinese is a man of relentless logic, and rational foresight is his forte. I even sense it in the tumbled picturesque market streets of Victoria, which straggle higgledy-piggledy up the lower slopes of the Peak, and are fragrant with soups when the sun goes down, but in which, I suspect, absolutely nothing is left to chance: and there is a bleak sense of order, too, to the industrial centres of the New Territories, where the powerful new factories, set in green gardens but towered over by chimneys, derricks and elevators, look like model factories in an exhibition. I am reminded sometimes of Rhodesia: not just in the newness, and the determination, but in a certain bland distortion of culture—as though Hong Kong is not quite true to itself, and lacks fizz accordingly.

I felt it on other levels, too. I went to a very grand dinner party one evening, and sensed it strongly there. The food was sumptuous, the service soft-footed, the conversation civilized. About half the guests were British, the other half Chinese, all well-heeled, all well-travelled, all equally Hong Kong: and after a while, I found, it was difficult to distinguish one from the other. They all spoke more or less the same upper-class English. They mostly shared the same kind of humour. They dressed alike, with slight cultural variations like split skirts or O.E. ties. It is true that one elegant young Chinese of indeterminate profession ('Well, I call myself a merchant on my passport—it sounds romantic, don't you think?') did admit to me that he sometimes felt isolated between the two cultures, but for the most part everyone seemed suavely at home on the cross-benches.

Yet I hope my host will not think me ungrateful if I say that the evening lacked fire. Perhaps they were all too alike? There was none of the mordant fun of a similar evening in India, say, where east and west parry each other with a wary and exhilarating love-hate. In Hong Kong the profit motive paradoxically defuses life, and makes nearly everyone brothers beneath the skin.

* * *

Yet I have a reservation at the back of my mind. It occurred to me that evening, as I contemplated my fellow guests, that the Chinese knew far more about the British than the British knew about the Chinese. The British had been on that coastline for 150 years, and had created Hong Kong: but in a deeper sense the Chinese had been there always. The British would mostly go home in the end, to Scotland or to Sevenoaks: the Chinese were there to stay. Few of the British spoke a Chinese language: all the Chinese spoke English. My merchant friend could doubtless have given me a fairly succinct account of, say, the difference between Presbyterian and Anglican: but no Briton there could have told me much about Taoism, or ventured to explain the nature of Chinese loyalty. The British of Hong Kong know a great deal about China as a trading opportunity, but when it comes to the profounder complexities of Chinese life, they are generally not much less ignorant than you or me.

Why should they be? They stick to their last, and this limited range of British vision suits the Chinese too. One feels in Hong Kong a sense of compromise. You mind your business, it seems to say, and I'll mind mine. The British seldom pry into the privacies of Chineseness: the Chinese do not often agitate for change. Almost everywhere in the old Empire foreign government came to be considered, rightly or wrongly, the worst sort of government there was. Not in Hong

Kong. Government is a chore there. Let the barbarians do it.

*   *   *

They do it well, but not of course perfectly. After a few days in Nathan Road I moved over to Hong Kong Island and put up at the Hilton. From my window there I looked down upon the Supreme Court, and often I observed there, in a space largely and freshly painted NO PARKING, the large black Daimler of the Chief Justice. The *South China Morning Post* noticed the car there too, while I was there, and photographed it in this self-incriminating station, but there was no response from His Honour, and the Daimler still stood there when I left.

It has not been suggested, I think, that in any larger way the judiciary of Hong Kong is corrupt. Its distinction is more doubtful. I went to court one day to watch the judges in action, and through all the usual flummery of English law, the wiggery and the pedantry, the royal ciphers and the stained mahogany, thought I detected up there on the bench no more than a provincial adequacy—unremarkable men, lucky (like most judges) to be elevated to such dramatic dignities, and living perhaps (like many expatriates) rather more loftily than they might at home. One does not, of course, expect brilliance from a colonial bench—a schoolmasterly fairness and honesty are all one can reasonably demand. In Hong Kong, though, a place full of brilliance, this judicial plod strikes one the more flaccidly, like a dollop of pastry in a rhubarb pie: and when I asked lawyers about it they ascribed it to a lack of incentive or opportunity among local Chinese to become judges themselves.

The reasons they gave were unimpeachable, and were concerned with salaries and legal education, but I could not help wondering if another cause might not be Hong Kong's infinite prospects of profitable mayhem, far more easily tapped by astute advocates than by honourable judges. Hong Kong is fearfully corrupt, and always has been. Before the last war the Government itself was involved in an intricate scandal—many a Hong Kong cupboard has its skeleton—and ever since the foundation of the colony the natural instincts of the place have bred skullduggery and intrigue. Hong Kong is one of the great drug entrepôts of the world; its protection rackets are ubiquitous; much of its daily life is based, in one degree or another, tacitly or explicitly, upon squeeze.

Hong Kong is touchy on the subject. The colony has had some

bad publicity lately, and the wise visitor, if she wishes to be invited to dinner next time, treads carefully around the subject of graft. 'You don't understand!' they say. 'This is Asia. Standards are different here. Compared with Saigon or Djakarta Hong Kong is lily-white!' The truth must be, though, now as ever, that Empire cannot have it all ways. If law and order is the speciality of the Raj, then it must honour its own standards. Old China hands may justifiably claim that Hong Kong, for all its myriad rackets, for all its 100 murders a year, for all its crooked policemen and opium entrepreneurs, is a more law-abiding city than most of its peers: admirers of the British tradition still expect higher standards of the last and greatest of the crown colonies.

Yet even as I write, I hear within my own mind charges of hypocrisy. I have always relished the freebooting side of Empire, the swashbuckle, the fur traders, the nabobs, the merchant adventurers. Yet what was that dashing enterprise but romanticized graft? I prefer to think of it as an eye for the main chance, but all too often it obeyed just the same principles as west African hash or Hong Kong tea money, and dealt often enough in the same commodities—'chasing the dragon', as the Hong Kong underworld still calls the pursuit of narcotics. Hong Kong is no more than a microcosm of imperial enterprise —good and bad in collusion, as they were in the old Empire itself.

*   *   *

I would guess that the vast majority of Hong Kong Government officials are there simply to do their best, while the vast majority of everybody else are there to get what they can. Opportunism is the *raison d'être* of Hong Kong, and virtually every private citizen of this colony is a speculator and a capitalist, from the richest developer to the poorest labourer.

I have observed some striking social contrasts in my time, *barriada* beside Lima penthouse, Rollses in Calcutta, oil sheikh and Bedu scavenger, but few have struck me as more curiously disturbing than the contrasts between Chinese rich and poor in Hong Kong. I am not sure why this is. It is not exactly a moral shock, for as I say virtually all Hong Kong people are animated by the same impulses, and the poor beggar would certainly be the swell investor if he could. It is certainly no post-imperialist shame: I am of the opinion that the British Empire has done well by Hong Kong, on the whole. Perhaps it is because the apparent homogeneity of the Chinese, their compact sense of racial power and superiority, somehow make disparities among them seem out of character. 'I believe the Chinese', wrote the British General Lord Wolseley in 1903, 'to be the most remarkable people in the world, and destined to be one of the master races.' The Chinese have some such effect upon most of us, and it is disconcerting to realize that they too have their winners and losers, their ups and their downs.

I felt this irrational shock most forcibly when I returned to Kowloon one afternoon after a visit to one of the settlement areas in the New Territories, where refugees from China proper are helped and housed. Out there a sense of barely escaped disaster informed the scene. The place was partly a housing area, partly a huddle of shacks, and it possessed all the trappings of twentieth-century calamity: the bundles of poor possessions, the ramshackle shelters of wood and canvas, the cluttered strings of washing in the tenement buildings, emaciated old people, pot-bellied young, hunger, bewilderment, good works, smells of dirt and open-air cookery, makeshift markets, bicycles, noise, congestion, runny noses—all the standard paraphernalia, in fact, of modern misery, translated this time into the Chinese idiom, and deposited upon the foreshore of Hong Kong. It was perfectly familiar to me. I had grown up with it, like any wanderer of my age, and it did not look out of place against the harsh rocky hillsides of Hong Kong.

But when I drove back to Kowloon I dropped into the Peninsula Hotel for tea, and there I discovered a Chinese contrast I had not experienced before. I was familiar enough, of course, with rich Chinese of the old kind, with collections of ivory carvings, and curly stone lions in their gardens: they offered no real contrast to the poor of the resettlement areas, but seemed to me of the same tradition, but temporarily more successful—exchangeable perhaps in the last resort, so that the beldams of the tenement could, given a damask dress and a pair of golden slippers, quite easily preside over the dinner table of the Victorian connoisseur. Now, however, ordering their cream cakes and India tea to the strains of Gershwin from the promenade orchestra, I observed an altogether new kind of Chinese upon display, so alien to those people of misery that for the first time I realized how fissiparous the Chinese civilization might be after all.

They frightened me rather, these new Chinese of the Peninsula. They had achieved some new synthesis of their own, freed from their own traditions but by no means subservient to ours. They were all young, and evidently rich, and they had to them a kind of stylized menace, suggestive of Kabuki more than Kung Fu. They were taller than Chinese used to be, and slinkier, and they were heavily made up, and wore fur fabric coats and many rings, and they dyed their hair in streaks, and sat slouched and disdainful in their chairs, reading *Time* magazine. The expression that our grandfathers used to call enigmatic seemed to have curdled, upon their faces, into an elegant sneer—for they *were* elegant, and handsome too, the girls languid and *svelte*, the men perhaps the first truly beautiful Chinese I had ever seen.

I encountered their kind often afterwards, making films, eating ice-creams, booking tickets to Zurich or sweeping in perfumed cars to floodlit race meetings. They came to dramatize for me the extreme nature of life in the colony, the violent range of the phenomenon. I sometimes went for my supper, if I had nothing better to do, to the open-air market beside the Macao ferry station, which springs up at sunset and provides a lively spectacle and an excellent cuisine—a bright hissing congeries of stalls, offering everything from monkey wrenches to Thai silks, and spilling hugger-mugger over the car park and across the road into the pavement of Connaught Road. I was always kindly welcomed there, and I generally ate a bowl of aromatic soup, piping hot, exquisitely spiced, nourishingly mucuous of texture and compounded chiefly of clams, crabs and bamboo.

One night, though, I decided to eat in my room, and consulting the Chinese menu always available at the Hilton Hotel, ordered a bowl of crab, clam and bamboo fungus soup. It arrived aromatic, mucuous and exquisitely spiced: but when I compared the price of it with the price of the soup at the market stall, identical in merit and if anything more generous in quantity, I found that the Hilton version cost just twenty-eight times as much.

*   *   *

Yet the balance holds, and I sometimes fancied in Hong Kong a sense of reconciliation—Asia and Europe come to terms. Thirty years ago, when Japan's Greater Prosperity Sphere reached across to Hong Kong, it seemed that Europe's day was ended on the China coast, and that Hong Kong would soon go the way of Weihaiwei, Shanghai and the other old footholds of the west. Even the Americans assumed, at the end of the Second World War, that Hong Kong would be returned to Chiang Kai-shek's China, and to many Britons too that seemed the natural course of events.

The loss of Singapore, in 1941, affected the British traumatically. It was the end of an age. The fall of Hong Kong, six weeks earlier, hardly seems to have affected them at all. By now the years of Japanese occupation seem almost forgotten even within the colony: the story is muffled, the tragedy muted, as though people wish not to be reminded of it. I drove out one day to the site of the Stanley prison camp, where most of the British population was confined for nearly four years, and where many died. The prison building is a prison still, and there are some sad tombstones in the graveyard along the road, crudely carved by the prisoners themselves in the midst of their misery: 'Skull of Unknown, December 1941', 'After Life's Fitful Fever She Sleeps Well', or 'K. S. Morrison, Chieftain, St. Andrew's Society'.

Even in Stanley itself, though, people responded vaguely, even evasively, to my questions: and when I called at the British Army camp which is still there, the soldiers at the guardroom seemed to think of the past as mere legend or superstition—'She's got hold of some information', they told the orderly officer, 'about this being where they interned people during the war'—and offered me only macabre and inaccurate anecdotes. I expected to experience some hush or charisma over a place that had seen so much suffering: but now the sun shone genially over the old compound, the air was fresh, the junks loitered prettily off shore, and even the spot where, thirty-five years ago, twelve Britons were beheaded for having a radio set, seemed to possess no air of elegy.

The Japanese left scarcely a mark behind them, except for the ugly tower they superimposed upon the Governor's palace, and they scarcely interrupted the progress of Hong Kong—which, in the resilient way of capitalism, resumed its affairs when they had gone almost as though nothing had happened. But the occupation did permanently affect relations between the British and the Chinese— between Britain and Asia, in fact. There lives in Kowloon an Irishman, a former member of the Hong Kong Government, who was exempted from internment by the Japanese because of his Irish nationality, and who advised the occupation authorities about the disposal of sewage, on which he was an expert. After the war, I am told, the British community, released from the torments of Stanley, reacted fiercely against this man, and he was forced out of the Government service, and ostracized by his colleagues. Today he is spoken of without resentment. His actions have fallen into a gentler perspective; the affront has been tempered by time; what once seemed treason to a cause, even a civilization, now seems little more than quixotry, or even common sense. The British in Hong Kong no longer seem to themselves to represent some other, superior order, some uncompromisingly separate set of values: if they have lost the imperial conviction, they have lost the delusions too.

Before the war their racial chauvinism was notorious. It survives still, of course, though chiefly in what British sociologists might call the lower middle-class expatriates, among whom, here as everywhere, a wog is still occasionally a wog ('They're no good,' one of those soldiers assured me, 'they don't *want* to understand, and they smell.') On more sophisticated levels I found no trace of it, unless you count bafflement as prejudice; on the contrary, I thought the British rather overdid their admiration of Chinese qualities, and could not help feeling, when inefficiently cheated by a kiosk girl, or unconvincingly blarneyed by a taxi-driver, that the Chinese sometimes underestimate us.

Certainly the community is full of Sinophiles. Some are scholars, devoted to the Chinese arts and sciences. Some just admire the industriousness of the race. Some, like me, respond to the almost Scottish mixture of kindliness and reserve so often to be discovered behind the Chinese mask. One well-known Hong Kong Englishwoman takes her bicycle to Peking for an annual holiday, and potters about the Celestial City sketching. An earlier generation of Britons was able to despise China, and to speak of Hong Kong as a notch cut by a woodsman on the trunk of China, to mark the spot for a later felling. Nobody can despise China now, and so one source of bigotry has been eliminated, to be replaced, if not yet by universal trust or affection, at least by a cautious respect.

Some Britons, following an old imperial tradition, have transferred their loyalties to Asia itself, and will live out their lives in Hong Kong. If anything, indeed, I found less resentment against Peking than against London. Like many another colony, Hong Kong is often at loggerheads with its distant Whitehall masters, especially perhaps when they are socialists, and what used to be called 'the imperial factor' irritates people as much on the Peak as it once riled Rhodes at Kimberley. In particular the issue of convertibility raises local tempers: London insists that Hong Kong's tremendous balances in London should remain in sterling, while the Hong Kong Government, like the Hong Kong banks, would like to diversify them into other, stabler currencies—to the detriment perhaps of sterling itself, but to the advantage of Hong Kong and its four million Chinese. I was reminded again of Rhodesia, at the time of U.D.I., and wondered if Hong Kong, too, was ever tempted to break away and constitute itself another city-state, like Singapore: but no, I was told, while Peking was prepared to tolerate a British Hong Kong, it would not stomach an independent Anglo-Chinese republic there on its very doorstep, like a nearer and still more equivocal Singapore.

Well, then, I used to ask, as a supplementary, was there no danger that the Chinese might, in one of their cyclic periods of aggression, simply march into Hong Kong anyway? 'Oh, I don't think so,' was the general tenor of the replies I got. 'That wouldn't be very civilized, would it?' This is the tenor of reconciliation: and those Britons who have elected to make Hong Kong their home for ever, and who have retired to villages on Repulse Bay, or are living out their years cherished by soft-footed familiars in tapestried apartments of the Peak— those who, by settling for ever in the colony, have become the first properly Hong Kong British, are staying there not because the island flies the British flag still, but because it is truly and irrevocably a corner of China.

*   *   *

A corner of China! Behind the relentless push of Hong Kong I often sense something gentler and more haunting: a yearning for China. It is not, obviously, a political yearning, nor even exactly a cultural urge, but only perhaps an instinctive impulse towards that mighty presence over the hills. China! If the name rings marvellously in London or New York, in Hong Kong, where the islands of the Kwangtung shore run away magically into the evening, where the junks chug in each morning from the Pearl River, where the acupuncture doctors practise their mysteries and the Chinese Merchandise Emporium offers you crystallized plums from Hunan—in Hong Kong the name of China is like the word of truth. China! It is the reality that underlies every illusion of Hong Kong, and even the Peak itself, that high place of western complacency, is really no more than an outcrop of the Kwangtung hills.

Before I left Hong Kong I drove out to Lok Ma Chau, on the frontier. This has become a famous tourist spot. The casual visitor is not allowed at the frontier post itself, beside the Sham Chun River, but a little way behind it there is an observation post upon a hill. There the Hong Kong Chinese have set up souvenir stalls and a café, and all day long a stream of visitors, mostly Japanese, steps out of its cars to wander up the winding path and gaze out to the north. The stalls offer a curious variety of wares, mostly from China proper: dingy postcards of Shanghai, table mats with Chinese horses on them, cheap jade bracelets, plaster figurines of ping-pong players, ideological tracts: but in the Chinese way the salesmen do not pester you as you pass on your way to the viewpoint. They know they can catch you on the way back.

It was a lovely day when I was there, and the view seemed almost complementary to the prospect my friend had offered me, two weeks before, looking over Hong Kong harbour from the top of the funicular. If that view was all punch, this was all pull. There across the river lay a silent country, green, blue and mauve—green for the paddy-fields that stained the wide plain, blue for the sheets of water that lay mirror-like beneath the sky, mauve for the hills of the horizon. China! It struck me not so much as peaceful or serene, as *simple*—innocent, perhaps. It looked like a world stripped of its pretensions and complexities, and as I stood there in the sunshine thinking about it for the first time I felt a stir of that yearning within myself, and found myself looking towards China as though that silent landscape were calling me home.

Home to where? Home to what? As I wandered down the track towards my car, one of the stall-sellers spoke to me quietly, without urgency, across his wares. 'Why don't you buy', he inquired, as though he genuinely, if mildly, wanted to know the answer, 'the thoughts of Chairman Mao?'—and he held up a small red book, bound in plastic.

'Get thee behind me,' I said.

A FANTASY OF GREATNESS

There is one place in Bath, and one only, where I sometimes feel that I am standing in a great centre of the European tradition. It is on the south bank of the river Avon, and it is best reached by walking up the river path beside the sports grounds. One passes then beneath North Parade Bridge, and emerging from its shadowy underside, fringed with ivy and ornamented by enigmatic graffiti, one sees suddenly the heart of the city gracefully disposed about its river.

The scene is dominated by the sound of it, for here the river flows frothily over a weir, and its perpetual hiss always makes me think of elaborate water-gardens in France or Austria, or the rush of greater rivers through cities of nobler consequence. To the left rises the square pinnacled tower of Bath Abbey, English Perpendicular in fact, but looking from this vantage-point squatter and stronger than it really is, and Romanesque in posture. In front is the exquisite fancy of Pulteney Bridge, with the windows of its shops opened over the water like a lesser Ponte Vecchio, and the heads of a tourist or two eating cakes in the Venetian Coffee Shop. On the left, above the wide belvedere of Grand Parade, the bulk of the old Empire Hotel is an unmistakable hint of Carlsbad or Baden-Baden. Gardens run down to the water's edge, with a floral clock and deck-chairs in them, and through the water-noise one can hear traffic on the street above, and perhaps the thump of a brass band. There is a steeple here, and a shallow dome there, and the brutal silhouette of a new tourist hotel shows inevitably above the bridge: and sometimes a man is fishing from a boat moored in the tumble of the weir, and there are pleasure-launches or barges moored beside the towpath. It is a scene that suggests grandeur and decision—symphony orchestras, influential newspapers, stock exchanges, parliaments perhaps. It feels as though up there above the river stands one of the European fulcra, where art and religion, history and economics combine to create a universal artefact, common to us all.

This is an illusion. Bath has never been a great city at all, and stands provincially aloof to the European mainstream. That river, which suggests Seine or Volga, rises in the Cotswold slopes twenty miles above, emerges into the Severn estuary fifteen miles below, and Bath too is small, inconsequential and altogether English. It is true that the Romans, exploiting the hot springs in this valley, made Aquae Sulis one of the best-known of their colonial spas, and that the medieval Abbey, like all the great English churches, grew up in close communion with its peers across the Channel. But Bath itself, Bath of the Georgian splendours, Bath of the golden stones and the Pump Room minuet, the Bath that Jane Austen knew and loathed, that Sheridan eloped from, that Gainsborough learnt his art in, that Clive, Nelson, Pope and Mrs. Thrale retreated to—Bath of the Bath buns and the Bath chairs, Bath of the dowagers, Bath that greets the visitor terraced and enticing as the train swings into Spa Station down Brunel's line from Paddington—the Bath of the persistent legend is a Somerset borough of the middle rank, rather bigger than Annecy, say, about the size of Delft. Its contacts with the greater world have been frequent, but tangential. A thousand years ago the first coronation of a King of all England took place in Bath, but since then the monarchs, the presidents and the premiers have come here only for pleasure, escape or lesser ceremony—an emperor in exile, a queen in search of pregnancy, a prime minister electioneering, a king comforting the victims of war.

Modern Bath is not, like those greater archetypes, an organic kind of city. Though it has existed on this site for nearly 2,000 years, the city we now know is more or less a fluke. For twelve centuries after the departure of the Romans it was an ordinary country town, distinguished from a thousand others only by the presence of the springs, and it was a sudden flare of fashion and fortuitous genius that made it, in the eighteenth century, a city *sui generis*. For forty or fifty years, perhaps, Bath was the most fashionable resort in England, and almost everything unique about it was created then, for a particular local purpose, mostly by local men. The publicists call it Bath, the Georgian City, but Georgian Bath was hardly more than a flash-in-the-pan—a craze, a passing enthusiasm, which soon petered out as crazes do, leaving the city to potter on once more as a bourgeois West Country town, known to the world chiefly for its Roman past and its literary associations, and inhabited in the popular fancy almost entirely by retired valetudinarians.

Yet that transient flowering of fashion has left behind it one of the most handsome cities in Europe, ironically preserved by its loss of glory. This is not, like Venice or Vienna, the capital of a vanished empire, or the seat of a discredited dynasty. One cannot mourn here forgotten kings, ruined bankers, defeated marshals. Bath's function was never very significant. People came here first to cure their agues, and then to have fun. There is nothing to be sad about, as we survey Bath's towers and trees across the river. The view may be evocative, but it is not in the least disturbing, for it is only a suggestion anyway, just as the bright genius of Bath is hardly more than a beautiful display, the whim or flourish of an era.

Walk on a little further, past the new floodgate, up the winding stone staircase beside the bridge; and on the road above you will find no horseback monuments of Habsburg or Bernadotte, only agreeable little shops, and a closer view of the tourists in the coffee shop, on their second cream slice by now, and petunias in wire baskets, and the piano showroom of Messrs. Duck, Son, & Pinker, and the gateway to the covered market behind the Guildhall, where Mr. Bennett is licensed to sell woodcock, snipe and venison, and Mrs. Reason offers her delectable and home-cooked pickled pork.

*　　　*　　　*

But if Power is not an attribute of Bath, Authority distinctly is— not the authority of political regimes, but the authority of manners. It is by no means a sanctimonious city: nineteenth-century Bath toughs were notorious, and Saturday night in Broad Street can still be a rumbustious celebration. It gives, though, an instant impression of order. Its very shape is logical. Its true centre, the Abbey churchyard, stands on the site of the original Roman temple, above the hot springs themselves. Around it in a circle lies the medieval city, within the circuit of its mostly vanished walls, and spreading away in all directions, up the Lansdown slopes to the north, up Bathwick, Widcombe and Lyncombe Hills to the south, along the line of the river east and west, Georgian, Victorian and twentieth-century Bath extends itself in terraces, crescents and respectable estates. It is a compact and manageable place. It has few sprawling suburbs, and its patterns are straightforward and easy to grasp.

The Romans, of course, brought their own method here, and the plan of their Bath, now mostly buried under the city streets, seems to have been functional to a degree, with its oblong temple precinct and its systematic bathing establishment, elegantly disposed about the shrine to Sul-Minerva, patron goddess of the site. But it was the eighteenth century which, deliberately copying Roman precedents, made Bath synonymous with rational design and integrated manners. The fashionable world then adopted the spa as a gambling centre, and London society flocked to its tables, bringing their vices with them: but the enlightened if ludicrous major-domo Richard Nash, a fastidious Welsh opportunist, so disciplined them into more reasonable behaviour that his Bath set the style of an age, and permanently affected the English balance of life. Under his supervision society restrained itself, tamed its horse-squires, brought its duchesses down to earth, until the middle and upper classes actually danced with one another, and the old hierarchy was discredited for good.

'Beau' Nash's autocracy of deportment was to be miraculously translated into the stone serenity that is the architectural glory of Bath. The city's great builders of the eighteenth century were frankly speculators, spotting and satisfying a market—most of their houses were lodging houses, to be let to families visiting Bath for the season. But their progenitor, John Wood the elder, was an antiquarian too, and in building his squares and terraces he drew upon older inspirations—on the Roman example, on the Palladian disciplines, even some suggest upon ancient schemes of prehistory, with their astronomically exact circles of stone, and their arcane but determined intentions. Georgian Bath became a city of right angles or gentle curves, uniform heights, uniform materials, built into its hillsides with a classical assurance, and sometimes even managing to look, in its long unbroken expanses of column and window, Druidically reticent. Nothing could be at once more controlled and more allusive than Wood's celebrated Circus, a perfect circle with three exits, its thirty-three houses decorated with a frieze of artistic, scientific and occupational symbols, lyres, masonic tools, the Aesculapian staff: and from the air Georgian Bath looks, with its geometric patterning, the perfect diagram of civic system.

Even the florid Victorians were restrained by the reasonableness of Bath, and in their passage through the city expressed themselves classically. The Kennet and Avon Canal, duck-haunted and lily-floated now, once the highway of coal-barges and lumber-scows, passed with a calm resolution through the southern part of the city, with its fine stone locks and its truly Roman passage beneath the structure of its own headquarters, Cleveland House—where a trapdoor in the floor, we are told, allowed the administrators to pass their instructions directly into the grimy hands of the bargees sweating beneath. When I. K. Brunel drove his broad-gauge track so magnificently down the Thames Valley, coming to Bath he did as the Romans did, building his bridges and culverts and tunnels in a grandeur of fine-dressed stone, sweeping gloriously beside the river, and only pausing with the waywardness of genius to build his Bath Spa Station in a sort of castellated Tudor.

Today Bath's authority is of a weaker kind, and expresses itself chiefly in mock-Georgian buildings of a flaccid inoffensiveness. Occasionally, though, one sees in the city streets, or waiting in the station forecourt, big black limousines with flagstaffs on their bonnets, driven by chauffeurs of faintly military mien, and stepped into, when the train comes in or the luncheon is over, by men of unmistakable command. You may suppose them to be successors in some sort to the old Beau, supervisors of the city manners: but no, they are the senior bureaucrats and occasional admirals of the Navy Department, several of whose branches settled in Bath for safety's sake during the war, and have been here ever since. They do impose order of a kind on Bath, though, for they provide the city's biggest industry, and give to their scattered premises, from the Empire Hotel which is their headquarters to the massed huts and car parks of Foxhill, a recognizably tight-lipped air. What is more, they have actually brought to Bath, if only in ellipsis, a true element of power: for it is here in the Georgian city of reason that the Royal Navy designs its nuclear submarines, which prowl the oceans perpetually on our behalf, and can obliterate almost anyone almost anywhere.

* * *

But there, no city could be much less warlike than Bath, and the Vice-Admiral who generally heads the Bath naval establishment is always a popular figure at Bath civic functions, addressing Rotary Clubs or presenting prizes. Anyway Bath depends far less upon its achievements than its people. Nuclear submarines apart, Bath has discovered a new planet (Uranus), devised a new shorthand (Pitman's), invented a new biscuit (Bath Olivers), fostered a masterpiece (*Tom Jones*), given its name to a bun and an invalid chair; but in general the city prides itself much more upon its illustrious visitors. Most celebrated Britons come to Bath at one time or another, and many distinguished foreigners too, but they have seldom done much in Bath—they have simply been there. The houses of Bath burgeon with plaques recording the residence of writers and admirals, empire builders and politicians, but often they only spent a season there in rented lodgings, recuperating for another battle, or correcting proofs.

Never mind, each left his trace behind him, however shadowy, and added a little to the mystique. I see them often, those elusive shades, as I wander the city. Miss Austen looks a little disgruntled as she picks her way between the puddles towards the circulating library. Lord Nelson looks a little wan as he opens his window in Pierrepont Street to see how the wind blows. Livingstone is pursued by admirers when he returns to No. 13 Royal Crescent, from his lecture at the Mineral Water Hospital. The great Duchess of Queensberry gasps, bursts into laughter and apologizes when Beau Nash tears her point lace apron from her waist and throws it to the ladies' maids. Pope limps through the gardens of Prior Park with his host, the Bath entrepreneur Ralph Allen, whose quarries provided the stone of Bath, and whose mansion magnificently surveys it. Sir Isaac Pitman scrupulously supervises the lettering, in his own phonetic script, on his new PRINTIN OFIS. Pepys taps his feet to the music of the peripatetic Bath fiddlers—'as good as ever I heard in London almost, or anywhere: 5s'. Wolfe, at his lodgings in Trim Street, opens the letter from London which will send him to victory and death at Quebec. The exiled Emperor of Ethiopia, bolt upright in a silken cloak, disappears like a wraith on the morning train to Paddington.

They come and go to this day, celebrities of every category, still to be seen spooning the raspberry sillabub at Popjoy's, or nosing in hired Daimlers around the Landsdown terraces. Bath views them with pleasure, but with detachment. There will always be others, and anyway citizens of Bath, like retainers at some princely household, keep their own character, live their own lives, unaffected by the passing of the great. More than most of the world's cities, Bath is familiar with fame, but in a very English way it remains in its deepest essence an ordinary provincial town: and though I know of few cities less anthropomorphic in character, so that I am never tempted to call Bath 'she', or give the place human qualities of its own, still it depends for its true flavour not upon those commemorative plaques or imaginary shades, but upon its own inhabitants.

Though Bath is magnificent, you will soon find that it is more homely than proud, its personality being at odds with its appearance. This is because the Bathonian is essentially a countryman still. The Bath dialect is roundly Somerset. The Bath face is unmistakably West Country, plump, genial. Nearly everyone remarks upon the gentle Bath manners—not exactly graceful, but nearly always kind. Bath is well stocked with country things, in from the country that day, Mendip cheeses, Somerset butters, wholemeal breads from Priston Mill, rough ciders, Cotswold vegetables. Even in the central parts of the city kitchen gardens flourish, horses, cows and sometimes even sheep graze. It is only twelve miles down the road to Bristol, that gateway to the Americas, but Bath feels a thousand miles from the sea and its affairs, and is essentially a country town still, where the green hills show at the end of the street, and the country people buy their tights at Marks and Spencer's.

Bath looks so patrician that many visitors suppose it to be socially glittering still, as it was when, during the brief kingdom of Beau Nash, society preferred his court to that of the King of England. It looks, after all, like a city of great town houses, attended by cottage streets and council flats for the domestics. But again it is illusion. Grand people live in Bath, people with butlers, people with titles, people with Rolls-Royces—people with shoe factories, or useful speculative properties in South London, or yachts in the Aegean. But they do not form a ruling caste, or even make one Bath address much better than another (though some of them would dearly like to). If you perambulate the city in the evening, peering through the half-drawn blinds and inspecting the names on doorbells, you will probably wonder what sort of people live in these parts: the answer must be—no sort. Bath still has its old-school trades-people, kindly maiden ladies in haberdashery, or elderly white-coated grocers who ask if they may deliver the cheeses, Madam, and there is to the very courtesy of its populace a faint suggestion of old precedences: but in fact the city is a social *mélange*, all its classes jumbled, none of its addresses exclusive, hippy beside general, writer below property tycoon.

There are the officials of the Navy Department, of course, whose senior officials form perhaps the most tightly knit community of Bath, and who tend to live in the country outside, or in the villa-country of the southern slopes. There is the usual layer of provincial worthies, the solicitors, the doctors, the businessmen and their wives who provide the municipal conscience, and cover the municipal perquisites, in any such town. Retired people traditionally come to Bath:

once they were likely to be rich West Indian planters, or East India merchants, and were buried beneath florid inscriptions in the Abbey, now they are usually pensioned and obscure, live among college crests or Ashanti shields in upstairs flats, and are interred in gloomy cemeteries.

There is an academic community, too, that emanates from Bath's technological university, and is inclined to inhabit bare rooms with Japanese lanterns and adjustable bookshelves—and a bearded and scrawny kind of hippy community which has made Bath a stopping place on the pilgrim routes to Glastonbury and St. Ives—and a growing number of people who have come to paint, write, sculpt and meditate in Bath—and lots of teachers from Bath's innumerable schools—and all the shopkeepers, of course, and the artisans, and the workers in Bath's light industries, who provide the true constants of Bath, whose fathers and grandfathers lived in the street before them, and who feel as though they have remained totally unaffected, cheerfully grinning from their cranes, taking tea-breaks on the front stairs, or explaining why it can't be done, come rain or shine, climax or decay, since they took over the place from the Romans.

In 1974 squatters moved into an empty house in the Royal Crescent, the haughtiest of the Bath terraces, and settled there making mildly revolutionary gestures. Some of the neighbours thought this the beginning of the end, but in fact the revolution came to Bath long ago. Occasionally, it is true, I do imagine its crescents peeling and unkempt under a philistine dictatorship, or forcibly converted into workers' holiday homes, and I seem to see the last of the admirals' widows scrubbing the floors of ideological museums, and those dear old grocers' assistants surreptitiously delivering black market butter to the back doors of lifelong customers. But I suspect it will never happen, for already the old structure is shattered, those aristocratic front doors are mostly no more than apartment block entrances, and the old styles linger on not as expressions of political form or social rigidity, but simply out of good country manners.

* * *

The hot springs of Bath, which gush from the ground at a temperature of 120° Fahrenheit, are the *raison d'être* of Bath. To understand what this means, one has only to go down to the Roman Baths, sunken among their perambulatories beside the Abbey, and enter the big bronze doors behind which the springs of Aquae Sulis still issue from the rock. By any standards of travel this is a profoundly moving experience, for men have been restoring themselves with these waters without a break for nearly two thousand years. THIS HOT SPRING USED BY THE ROMANS, says an inscription above the door, HAS BEEN FROM TIME IMMEMORIAL THE PRINCIPAL SOURCE OF THE HEALTH-GIVING WATERS OF BATH. The air is hot and clammy in there, the steam billows, but there is to that dark grotto a wonderful suggestion not merely of age, or continuity, but of solace.

Solace, in one form or another, is the truest purpose of Bath. Legend says that Prince Bladud, a hazy prince of the Britons, discovered the healing properties of the Bath springs when his leprous swine wallowed in the mud of this valley. Certainly the Romans soon discovered both the pleasures and the cures of the waters, and Aquae Sulis became a health resort well known throughout the western Empire. Though the baths themselves fell into ruin under the Saxons, and were not excavated until the nineteenth century, the springs were never forgotten: throughout the centuries of Bath's obscurity people drank and bathed in them—Charles II came in 1677, James II in 1687. One of Bath's most popular souvenirs is a print of the baths in 1675, a Hogarthian scene of squalor and vivacity, men, women and children all in the pool together, some naked, some ridiculously clothed, floating on their backs, splashing each other, diving off the conduit, while from the windows of the surrounding houses, from the balconies, all around the balustrade, the yokels of the city idly gawk. 'Methink', wrote Pepys in 1668, 'it cannot be clean to go so many bodies together in the same water.'

Directly from the waters, too, sprang the eighteenth-century climax of Bath, though now the search for bodily health or vigour was diversified into a quest for pleasure. Bath was a place for gambling and dalliance, promenade and theatre, as well as a spa. Beau Nash was one of the sponsors of the Mineral Water Hospital, but he was far more concerned with the social life of Bath than its medical system, and so were most of his clients. Theirs was a solace of the spirit, and today too, though the Royal National Hospital for Rheumatic Diseases still pipes the waters to its treatment rooms, though Bath is full of prosperous doctors, and though most self-respecting visitors to the Pump Room take a dubious sip from the conduit ('wery strong flavour o' warm flat-irons,' Sam Weller thought), still the best purpose of the modern city is simply to give delight.

Like most pleasure-cities, Bath can be uncommonly displeasing, mostly by contrast. When the weather is wrong, or the mood jars, even the splendours of the place go sour. Then the honey-gold turns to grey, the hills look drab and lifeless, the young people seem to disappear from the streets, and Bath seems despondently sunk in its muggy valley—its sulphurous pit, as Pope called it. It can be a claustrophobic city: the hot springs underground, perhaps, give it a stifling feeling, and the orderly ranks of its terraces can look heartless and impersonal, standing there door by door in the drizzle.

But catch the right day, the right wind, and then Bath can be the very happiest city in England. Then the crescents and squares look no longer regimented, but benign and comradely. Then the grey deserts the stone, and the gold creeps back. The average age of the populace seems to drop by twenty years or so, the tables outside the pubs are full and lively, long skirts swish down Milsom Street, guitar music sounds from the upstairs pads of Park Street. Bath seems full of flowers then, and the little pedestrian alleys in the city centre are bright with fruit, trendy clothes and *Private Eye*, and on the green below the Royal Crescent the small boys of the Jamaican community set up their stumps and play deft and hilarious cricket in the sun.

Then the order of the place becomes not an imposition, but a liberation. As the black of a dinner-jacket sets off the bright colours of a dress, so the squares, crescents, quadrangles and circles of Bath provide a grand geometric stage for the flow of life that passes through it. Against such an imperturbable background, almost anything goes better: a military tattoo, a car rally, an outdoor performance of Molière, cricket, throwing frisbees, eating pork pies in pub gardens— Bath has the gift of heightening all activities, and giving an unexpected beauty to everyday affairs. If I am having trouble with a recalcitrant paragraph, I simply go outside and wander through the town for half an hour: and the proportions of the place, the green interventions, the honey-stone and the gentle faces soon put my adjectives in order, and calm my restless cadences.

*   *   *

This recuperative power resides partly in the manner of Bath—a smooth, bedside manner that is set by its Georgian dominants. It is a densely built city—no more than a couple of miles across, and rounded —and like many of the greatest architectural ensembles, like the cities of inner Spain, or the prairie clusters of the American West, its best parts have an oddly portable feel to them. So dexterously fitted are their sections to one another, so organically embedded in their setting, that one feels they could be prised *in toto* from their environment, and lifted for closer examination. All around the countryside shows, wherever you look, and this green frame accentuates the easy unity of Bath, too, as the sea undeniably gives extra point to an island.

Because of the narrow scale, the beauty of Georgian Bath depends heavily upon perspective. Depth and vista are essential to these buildings, and no city is more vulnerable to the distortion of the telephoto lense. Built on flat ground, Bath would lose half its fascination: its architectural emphasis is mostly horizontal, and the rolling hills around, the gradual slope towards the river valley, the rich green trees of park and garden, provide the necessary uprights. But there is no hint of *trompe-l'oeil* to the great buildings of Bath. They are rational, gentlemanly, straightforward buildings, thoroughly English, whose effects are achieved not by deceit, but by relationships.

One of the delights of Bath is the shift of its planes, building against building, street behind street, as though some master producer is juggling with his stage sets. Because it is not truly a great city, powerful of meaning or intent, the pace of this architectural parade can be light-hearted. One does not wish to hurry a Paris or an Edinburgh, solemn as they are with memories of faith and history, or even a New York, where humanity itself seems to have reached some kind of frenzied apotheosis. But Bath is only for fun, and anyway is so small that one can always come round a second time, so that for myself, though I love to walk about the city, I think it displays itself best of all from the windows of a slowly moving car. Then the surprises and entertainments of the place, which are essentially frivolous, move at the right cheerful pace. The smooth lines of the city masonry glide along un-jogged, the crescents slide by with the proper sensuous motion, and the serendipities of Bath fall thick and fast.

Of these the most celebrated occurs at the end of Brock Street, on the lower slope of Lansdown. It is among the most famous of architectural surprises, and provides one of the happiest moments of European sight-seeing. I experience it myself a couple of hundred times a year, but I never tire of it. This Bath moment especially is best observed by car, and I like to do it with the roof open and something blithe and brilliant on the tape—Mozart, Mendelssohn, or Astaire singing Cole Porter. Then I swing exuberantly around the Circus, beneath the marvellous centrepiece of planes (cocking a snook as I go at those grim purists who would chop them down for architecture's sake), and head down the short, straight link road called Brock Street. I pretend I have never been there before, and for visual reasons drive slap down the middle of the street. At the end there seems to be a vacancy—cloud, trees, a snatch of green, the corner of a large house protruding slightly in the middle distance, a transverse terrace beyond. Is it a park? Is it a football ground? Is it a demolition site? The plan gives nothing away; the vacancy remains vacant; only that sense of impending space grows as I approach the end of the road; and then, narrowly avoiding the Mini which, in a less exuberant condition, emerges aghast from Church Street, I top the barely perceptible rise, ease myself around the corner, and find before me one of the most splendid *tours de force* of European design, the Royal Crescent.

It lies there in a shallow arc, its wide lawns running away beyond the ha-ha down the hill below, and all is suddenly space, and green, and leisure. Though the Crescent is architecture on a truly palatial scale, and reminds many people of Versailles, to me it suggests far more pungently the seaside. It is like the grandest of all rows of seaside villas, standing on a promenade before a sea of grass: the children bathe on the green below, the householders walk their dogs along the beach, and the sign that enjoins No Organized Games is merely a delicate way of saying that if you are looking for What The Butler Saw, try the pier. I have seen visitors stopped in their tracks as, turning that same corner of Brock Street, they have discovered this glorious scene in front of them: and the look of astonished delight upon their faces is just the look the holiday-makers have when, tumbling from the train and walking down Beach Street from the station, they have reached the esplanade that is their destination, and see the sands, all balloons, whelks and motor-boat trips, there in the sun before them.

*   *   *

No *trompe-l'oeil*: but if the charm of Bath is not deceptive, it is unexpectedly intricate. It relies upon contrast, for all among those splendid set-pieces, wedged in here and there, corners of quirk or curiosity provide a filigree. Narrow steps and alleys lead the eye to greater spectacles; railings, brackets, details of stone and ironwork throw into grander relief the classical frontages behind; artisan cottages correct the scale of things; grace-notes relieve the splendour. Symmetries are broken. Incongruities occur. Much of this complicated sub-Bath, the civic undergrowth, has lately been destroyed, sometimes for good social reasons, more often because of planners' *naïveté*, developers' greed and architects' sterility. Just enough remains to preserve the flavour. There are enclaves of petty Georgian, like Beaufort Square, behind the Theatre Royal, which possesses a crooked, almost edible allure, as though all its little houses are made of pastry. There are follies, like Beckford's Tower on Lansdown Hill, or Allen's Sham Castle across the valley. There are streets like Walcot Street, beside the river, which begins with a bang in the jolly Hat and Feather, ends in a whimper with the hapless new Beaufort Hotel, but contains in its short length a heady jumble of chapels, terraces, junk shops, hippy hang-outs, derelict gardens, old steps, gates that go nowhere, cul-de-sacs, an arcaded corn market, a green graveyard—the whole made fragrant by the smell of new bread from the Red House Bakery and raw meat from the cold storage depot, and sneeringly overlooked by the immense curve of the Paragon above.

Take Lansdown Crescent, which stands regally on the upper Lansdown slopes, white-painted and festively illuminated by its own wrought-iron gate lamps. Lansdown has more panache than the Royal Crescent, with its undulating double curves and its rising and falling ground, but it is still very magnificent, and stylishly inhabited. Butlers and judges are to be found in these fine houses, rich manufacturers, bankers' widows, art historians. One house is furnished basement to attic entirely in the Georgian mode, and to the house once inhabited by the mystic Francis Younghusband a hardly less visionary American has brought a new kind of civilized living to Bath, part Japanese, part Manhattan, with a square sunken bath in the Roman kind, and a carpeted, sun-decked penthouse of delightful indulgence.

Yet this famous crescent is embedded in crinklier matter. Directly in front of those magnificent houses, an unkempt meadow tumbles steeply down the escarpment, infested by nettles and thistles, and grazed by horses, heifers, sometimes even sheep. Directly behind them, a gnome-like settlement flourishes. There are converted stables with creepers winding round their drain-pipes, and little cobbled yards with children's tricycles in them, and ivy-locked garden gates, and damp dead-end passages, and apple-trees, and motor-scooters in sheds, and summer-houses through whose windows, impenitently peering, one may discover half-completed water-colours, animal skulls, old pianos or book-presses. It is like another country back there, or a colony of churls and craftsmen in the purlieus of a princely court.

Or consider the piazzetta at the heart of Bath—the Abbey churchyard, site of the altar of Sul-Minerva, which one best enters under the colonnade from Stall Street. This lies in the middle of Bath's downtown circumstance, such as it is. One side of the little square is formed by the façade of the Pump Room, another consists of eighteenth-century shops, and the end is blocked by the imposing west front of the Abbey, with its huge carved door and its angels tumbling up and down their ladders to heaven.

It is quite a noble arrangement, but if the frame is monumental, the scene is miniature—like a toy piazza. On a summer day its benches are usually crowded with tourists, shoppers and idlers. A little bar is set up in the shadow of the colonnade, with sun-shades and rows of bottles, and groups of very foreign visitors wander in and out of the Pump Room doors, in and out of the dark Abbey, gazing into the souvenir shops or wondering whether to commission a plaque to their family arms from Mr. Howe on the corner. It is, though, fundamentally a domestic scene. The Abbey front towers above it all, but still there are prams about, and housewives gossiping over their coffee. You can have your hair done here, or order a pair of spectacles, and above the premises of Alfred Shore & Sons ('Distinction in Dress Shoes') one may sometimes see Mr. Greenwood the dentist actually at his drill. Napoleon called St. Mark's Square the finest drawing-room in Europe, but the Abbey churchyard is no more than the most agreeable parlour in England, a little place, an intimate place, a place to chat or sew in, or decide what to get for supper.

*　　*　　*

There is a poignancy to this diminutive side of Bath, or if not a poignancy, a wistfulness. Come inside the Pump Room, now. The Pump Room Trio is performing, as it does every weekday morning, and the handsome room is full of visitors, drinking fairly muddy coffee, sampling the spa water from the tap in the bay window, or looking down to the water of the King's Bath outside. Kindly waitresses bustle about, the tall Tompion clock ticks away against the wall, Beau Nash stares superciliously from his statue in its niche. The musicians play on stage behind a palisade of geraniums, potted palms on a balcony above their heads, and I often go down there to enjoy their company, correcting a manuscript over my coffee, or just observing the scene. It is not only that they play 'Rosemarie', 'Oklahoma' or 'Perchance to Dream' with a splendid enthusiasm: it is also because they seem to represent a culture that has almost died—a lost, innocent culture, fitfully and nostalgically surviving here. They must be almost the last café trio still performing in Great Britain; I take many visitors to hear them, and they often make a deeper impression than the Roman Baths.

This is a melancholy pleasure, but then some of Bath's fascination is melancholy. Before the Second World War it was a much sadder place than it is now, and old photographs show it drab, blackened and down-at-heel, even its prodigies looking sadly neglected, and its detail obscured with dirt and excrescences. But even today, though most of it is spick and span, it often has a sadness to it. People analyse this in different ways. Some think it is just nostalgia for the eighteenth century, which seems so close in Bath, but is really so far away. Some put it down to the climate, which can be horrid. Some again are depressed by the introspective feel of the place, or are enervated by the uniformity of its stone. Some dislike its museum feeling. Some are desolated by its changes, and one or two I have met are placed at a particular disadvantage by their distaste for Georgian architecture.

I myself attribute the sensation to an unfulfilment in Bath. Since the end of the eighteenth century, and the departure of the fashionable to newer and racier resorts, Bath has never recaptured its purpose—or rather, the particular purpose that the Georgians gave it, and for which their glories were designed. Bath is only a bourgeois Somerset town, dressed like a capital: a city built for art and pleasure, trying to be a Regional Shopping Centre. There are attempts to make it more—the Festival of the Arts, the Arts Workshop, the Bath Preservation Trust, the American Museum. Bath has many devoted amateurs, and several well-intentioned patrons. The City Fathers, though, are reluctant to accept its hedonist place in the world, so that it remains something of a façade. Its palaces are not palaces, only blocks of flats. Its Abbey is only a parish church. Its Festival happens once a year, and when it is over the performers and choreographers, arrangers and composers disperse again, leaving the city to the Pump Room Trio and the electronic organ in the Parade Gardens.

The backs of Bath buildings are very revealing. A few of the swankiest terraces are grand behind too, but for the most part Bath's builders did not much care about rear elevations, and successive improvers and developers have stuck their additions haphazardly on the back walls, giving half Bath a hodge-podge, job-lot look which I particularly like. The back of Marlborough Buildings offers one such spectacle. This is a large range of terrace houses, built speculatively in the late 1780s. From the front it looks decorous, especially No. 9 (where I live). From the back it looks an enthralling muddle. There are allotment gardens back there, and if you stroll among their beans and chrysanthemums, looking up to the massive wall of masonry above, the effect is troglodytic. It is as though a natural rock-face stands there, pitted with the thousand caves and burrows that are its windows. There are thirty-three houses in the row, and from the back all look different. Some have six floors, some five. Some are impeccably maintained, some look like slums. Their windows are splodged or hacked almost indeterminately across the cliff, and there are balconies stuck on here and there, and outhouses, and jutting alcoves like Turkish *mahrabiyas*, and sham windows here, and blocked doors there, and racks for flower-boxes, and washing-lines, and sometimes the curtains look richly velvet, and sometimes they appear to consist of a couple of discarded blankets strung up on cord.

In another city those little private havens would be full of purpose, and Marlborough Buildings does of course house its quota of business people, civil servants, students, even a writer or two. But Bath lacks the tautness of a truly functional city, a city that fits its own buildings, and when I stroll back there in the evening I often think what a melancholy diffusion of energy that cliff face represents. How many of those windows, I think, represent not a purpose, but a lack of it! Widows, childless divorcees, elderly unmarried ladies, dilettanti, pensioners, the retired—Bath is full of lonely people without occupations, counting the days until their grandchildren come to call, killing the evening with television, gin or marijuana, plotting another bridge party, waiting for bingo, or setting off down the hill for an hour with the Pump Room Trio. Every city has its share of the purposeless, but by the nature of things Bath has more than most, and the saddest of the bell-push names, I think, are those whose faded pride lives on in a polished but almost indecipherable brass plate, or a visiting card engraved in the deep copper-plate of long ago.

This human emptiness has its physical counterpart too. If much of Bath is newly restored, much is hangdog still. There are houses never rebuilt since the blitz, or awaiting, year after year, planning permission or builders' cash. There are abandoned churches up for sale. Through the cracks of stately flagstones tufts of grass spring through, and sometimes the corner of a garden, the elbow of an alley, is choked with creeper and bramble, as though a civilization has retreated here, and the weeds are taking over. It is another illusion of course—Bath is in better shape than it has been for many decades: but still the tristesse is real, in this city that is too splendid for itself, and often it creeps through Bath in the late afternoon, or one awakes to find it hanging over the city like a cloud, deadening the repartee of the milkman, and sending many of the old ladies, I suspect, sensibly back to bed again.

*   *   *

I am thinking chiefly of public Bath, prodigy Bath, those districts of the city that were specifically built for its eighteenth-century climax. Elsewhere, of course, the older, more modest functions of the town survive as always, and all the structure of an English country borough has been handed down undisturbed from the Middle Ages. One pleasant way to sense this other Bath, I think, is to desert the Lansdown slopes and the city centre, where the tourists swarm, and cross the river, the railway and the canal to the hills of the southern side. Here is another city altogether, hardly less beautiful in its less showy way, and closer perhaps to the inner spirit of the place, which has resisted so many shifts of fortune, and remains essentially quiet and countrified.

There are terraces over there, and cottages, and new housing estates, and there used to be some fairly rugged slums, but it is above all villa country on the slopes of the southern hills. Scattered through the trees towards Claverton scores of half-Italianate, half-Regency villas stand among their gardens, some luxurious, some modest, all very private. They are lived in by families, most of them, not divided into flats, and they retain a sprightly and comfortable air. They are not show houses. They are real. Children play in their gardens, and the paterfamilias drives home from the office in his Rover. Here one realizes the true social condition of Bath: an unexceptionable country town beneath it all, with its own private pedigree of burgher, tradesman and labourer, its own civic preoccupations, its own narrow coteries and rivalries, come legionary, come Beau.

Only the presence of lost genius makes it special, elevating it to a status far above itself, and the best place of all, I think, to enjoy this pungent and ironic state of affairs, where the ordinary meets the superb, the parochial touches the international, is at Widcombe, in the heart of the villa country. This is one of those ancient country hamlets which have been absorbed into the fabric of the city, and it is recognizably a village still, with its church, its manor house and its village war memorial. Widcombe feels immensely old, and stable in a rural way, as though it recognizes deep in its stones and roots that the business of life is living itself.

Beside the church a lane leads steeply up the hill. It meanders on for a couple of hundred yards, and then comes to a halt at an iron gate beside some cottages. To my mind this is the most Bathonian place in Bath, truer by far to the city's spirit than that metropolitan view beside the river, and more telling than any contrived delight of the Lansdown crescents. The cottages beside you are true country cottages, *rus in urbe*, with moss-grown steps and cherished vegetable gardens. Green fields rise all about, giving the dell a properly nooky feel, and through the gates one may see a gamekeeper's cottage, and a sedgy lake with swans, ducks and moorhens in it.

It is a gentle scene, part country, part town, and unpretentiously assured: but beyond the lake there stands something very different— the exquisite little Palladian bridge, roofed and pillared, built long ago for the delectation of Ralph Allen, when he walked with his guests in his mansion high above. It is a little golden structure, all by itself in the green, which stands there with an air of mock innocence, but which speaks of Rome and Vicenza, Pope and Goldsmith, minuets and royal visits, and all the heady ideas, idioms and experiences which have, down the centuries, brought to this modest English town a fantasy of greatness, and by fostering it with such grace, fun and harmony, made the illusion true.

FAME'S STAMPING GROUND

Failing to solve any of the problems in the airline magazine's puzzle page, and soon exhausting all the faces upon which I could superimpose buck-teeth or incongruous side-burns, as we approached Washington, D.C. I turned to that beloved stand-by of the experienced traveller, the Application for Diners' Club credit cards. With a practised hand I registered my name as Ethelreda B. Goering, my Amount and

Source of Other Income as eight million dollars, Gold Mine, Transvaal, and as we landed I was delightfully debating whether to use as my Personal Reference His Holiness the Pope, Windsor Castle, Lhasa, or J. P. Morgan at the University of Lapland.

Imagine then my pleasure when, arriving at my hotel that evening and opening the Washington Directory, I discovered the Mayor of Washington to be Mayor Washington, the Treasurer of the White House Correspondents' Association Mr. Edgar A. Poe, and the Doorkeeper of the House of Representatives Mr. William (Fish Bait) Miller. A concomitant of power is the privilege of eccentricity, and though in recent years Americans may have pined for rulers of more orthodox method, still to visitors from smaller and less potent states an early intimation of quirk is more a comfort than a threat—the gods make their victims mad, but their favourites unconventional.

Besides, it has a healthily deflationary effect upon the stranger. The great Muslim travellers of the Middle Ages, when they approached the capital of some unimaginable Caliph or omniscient Sultan, fell as a matter of form or policy into a special ceremonial prose, matching their cadences to the Master of the World, or adjusting their punctuation to the Commander of the Faithful. I had wondered myself, as I set off for Washington this time, what avedictory style might be best suited for the current Sublimity of the White House. When I first came to the city President Eisenhower sat in the Hall of a Thousand Ears, and his style was easily, as you might say, approximated to. President Kennedy no less obviously demanded a mixed pastiche of Hemingway, Tolkien and Zane Grey, while President Nixon, of course, could only in courtesy be addressed in his own meaningful communicational media.

But President Ford offered the pilgrim no text. Something faintly sanctimonious, perhaps? Something brisk and sporting? Something bland, something soothing, some literary equivalent of orange juice or rub-down, to honour his role as the Great Jogger? I could not make up my mind: and so, abandoning the precedents of Ibn Khaldun and Ibn Batuta, and encouraged by the evidence of the Washington Directory, I decided to skip the honorifics altogether, and simply say Hi to Fish Bait—who turned out to be, by the way, an inescapable figure of Washington life, and who earned his nickname, so his office told me, during a shrimp- or worm-sized boyhood on the Mississippi shore.

*   *   *

Unreality, of course, whether comic, paranoic or simply bizarre, is an attribute of capital cities, because power itself is so illusory. We look on the face of Nixon as of Ozymandias, and even Harun al-Rashid survives only in the fancy of his story-tellers. At least, though, the Caliph could disguise himself when he wished, and walk anonymously through the market-place of Baghdad, where the poets declaimed, the merchants haggled and all jostle of the real world was available outside his palace gates. When President Nixon wished to do the same, he could only go to the Lincoln Memorial, slightly drugged it seems, and talk to the tourists in its sepulchral glow.

The idea of an artificial capital is, I believe, specifically American, though the nature of Washington is of course another legacy of those damned French. It was a rotten idea, disastrously copied in such dumps as Canberra, Brasília and Islamabad, and inevitably creating in the nation's capital just the same blinkered introspection as one finds in new universities started from scratch on virgin rural sites. But though everyone claims to miss the stimulus of variety in Washington, like academics politicians are terrified of outside competition, so that in practice all conspire to maintain the shrine-like posture of the place. It is a posture, altogether spurious, of dedicated zeal and memorial— a necromantic attitude, in fact, sustained by the commanding presence of the Arlington National Cemetery, Fame's Camping Ground as it says on its triumphal arch, and suggesting to me sometimes, not least when the carillon of the Union Mission Center rings out its hymns twice daily across the Mall, the hush of elegy that one still feels in the heart of Hiroshima (though I was sorry to discover, when I inquired at the Mission door, that there was in fact no glazed lady carillonist playing 'Abide With Me' in the roof, only a man in shirt-sleeves with a tape recorder at the reception desk).

From the centre of that allegoric cemetery one may look out across the Potomac to the grand sweep of the capital beyond. Nothing could appear much less American, for while America is above all a country of verticals, artistic, economic, symbolic, phallic, imposed splendidly upon the passive landscape, Washington, D.C. is all horizontal. Nowhere is much flatter than Washington. The ground is flat. The style is flat. The architecture is deliberately flat. From up there in the Arlington Cemetery the whole city seems to lie in a single plane, without depth or perspective, its strips of blue, green and white, layered along the river, broken only by the obelisk of the Washington Monument and the Capitol Dome as the massed ranks of Arlington are interrupted only by the graves of specially important corpses. It looks like a city of slabs, reverently disposed: and only the jets from the National Airport, straining themselves with difficulty out of the ambiance, throw a bold diagonal across the scene.

'Are all these,' said a child to me outside Arlington House, surveying Fame's Camping Ground around us, 'are all these *dead* guys?' 'Dead,' said I, 'as mutton'—but at that moment her grandmother arrived, direct I would guess from Kalamazoo, and throwing me a distinctly accusatory look, as though I were undermining the loyalty of the young, she gave the child's nose a necessary wipe of the Kleenex, and hurried her down the hill to catch the Tour-Mobile.

* * *

The sentries at the Tomb of the Unknown Soldiers are mounted by an infantry regiment known as the Old Guard, and for myself I found them more haunting than the shades. I suppose new arrivals at Arlington are, so to speak, cosmeticized before burial, but however assiduously they are touched-up for their last roll-call, they could hardly be more theatrical than those soldiers still alive. Apparently shaven-headed beneath their peaked caps, ominously sun-glassed when the day is bright, expressionless, ritually stooped, they move with an extraordinary gliding motion that seems to require no muscular activity at all, but is controlled electronically perhaps from some distant command post—a slow, lunar motion, to and fro before the gaping crowds—a halt, a click of the boots, a stylized shift of the rifle from one shoulder to the other, a long pause as though the electrodes are warming up, and then, with an almost perceptible buzz, that slow spectral lope back to the other side of the memorial, while the tourists suppress a shudder.

Behind their dark glasses, I suppose, the soldiers know nothing of the sinister chill that surrounds them, and indeed when I later came across some of the Old Guard off-duty at their barracks, they seemed nice cheerful fellows. In the same way the obsessive nature of Washington is not always apparent to those who form part of it. 'When I was just a little kid,' a friend of mine told me at lunch one day, 'I guess I wasn't more than six or seven years old, I used to dream to myself I could see my name there on the bedroom door—Senator W——!' I could hardly conceive such a fancy in a child's mind, but she saw nothing remarkable about it, and it is probably commonplace in Washington. Politicians are politicians everywhere, but only here is the political addiction so ingrained and so frank. Here one can observe its pursuit in every fanatic detail, from the dream of the visiting debating society president to the attendant hush when the great man speaks, from the swivelling eye over the canapés to the sweep of the big black cars at the Senate side.

To avoid getting hooked myself, for it is catching as well as habit-forming, sometimes I took the day off from politics, and did the tourist rounds: but for all the grandeur and meaning of the city, for all the endearing pride of my fellow visitors, still these experiences only heightened my sense of intrusion upon some immense private performance. Inorganic by origin, Washington is unnatural in behaviour: but far from heightening everything as New York does, it spreads everything out, memorializes it, puts it in a park and reflects it in an ornamental pool. In New York I feel more myself than usual, in Washington much less, for when I look for my own reflection in this city, statues and symbols look back at me.

It is an alienating city. It lacks the corporate gift of hospitality. It is like one vast smokeless zone. Was ever genius less at home than in the National Gallery of Art, where the enigmatic Giorgione, the mad Van Gogh, the lusty Picasso hang for ever antiseptically among the Garden Courts? Did ever Marlowe or Molière find a less likely stage than the Center for the Performing Arts, which suggests to me a cross between a Nazi exhibition and a more than usually ambitious hair-dresser? I thanked my good fortune that this time I had arrived in September; at least those interminable cherries weren't in blossom.

Nowhere in the world is so inexorably *improving*. Elevating texts and aphorisms, quotations from statesmen and philosophers, Thoughts for All Eternity nag one from every other downtown wall, and make one feel, especially perhaps if one has come in a High School excursion bus, awfully insignificant. What giants there were in those days! How grandly they expressed themselves! How thickly they stand about! Innocent III, Napoleon, Blackstone and St. Louis supervise the Senate subway; clumps of heroes wrestle with their standards, horseback generals revise their strategies, on plinth and plaza across the capital. 'Where Law Ends', booms the Department of Justice, 'Tyranny Begins'. 'Taxes Are What We Pay For A Civilized Society', retorts the Internal Revenue Service. 'Here Are The Ties That Bind The Life Of Our People', the National Archives cry, and across the avenue the Mission responds, with a chime of the carillon: 'Come To Me!'

When we came down from the top of the Washington Monument, even the elevator operator dismissed us with a parting injunction. 'Let's all work', he said, 'to clean up our country for the 200th anniversary just coming up.' 'Yes sir,' we dutifully replied, 'you're darned right—you hear that, kids?' He had not, however, finished yet. 'And I'm talking,' he darkly added, 'about the mental aspects as well as the physical.'

We had no answer to that.

* * *

Let me insert, if you will forgive me, two anecdotes of Westminster Abbey. One I report first-hand. I was standing once in a cluttered alcove of the fane, romantically topsy-turvy with statues of forgotten admirals, judges and miscellaneous rulers of the world, when I heard behind me the comment of an American visitor. 'All it needs', she observed *sotto voce* but decisively, 'is a good museum curator from the Middle West.' A second quotation was given me by one of the Abbey's guides. 'Sir,' another American remarked politely to him one morning, 'it occurs to me that this building looks remarkably like a church.'

I throw them in because I am aware of a prejudice in my reaction to the Washington aesthetic. I stand with Chesterton for the rolling road, and prefer even the symmetry of the Greeks or the Georgians to have its nooks and serendipities. This is, I know, a taste common in my own particular culture, but rarer elsewhere, and one must bear in mind that the singular beauties of Washington, more than the beauties of less significant cities, lie in the eyes of their beholders. I can see that, for example, the motto inscribed on the Seabees Memorial— *Can Do*—which seems slick or cheap to me, translates with perfect dignity as *On Peut*, and to a visitor from Rome, Lyons or Castile the Beaux Arts monumentality of Washington is no doubt only to be expected. We all see ourselves in America, and we see our own countries, our own civilizations, confirmed, denied or parodied in Washington, D.C.

The fantasy of the place is nourished, indeed, by the foreigners who frequent it. The presidents and prime ministers who succeed each other day by day at Blair House are like pilgrims come to consult the great oracle across the way. The embassies strung out among their flags and gardens on Massachusetts Avenue are pavilions of make-believe. It is all a parade! The Shah is indistinguishable from the Chairman, to the maid who makes their beds. The embassies are built on air, with their agency-supplied man-servants or KGB-men in disguise, their government-issue carpets or regulation ikon, their signed portraits of king or dictator among the dahlias on the grand piano, their ineffable hostesses, their suitable oil paintings, their envoys brought to this heady eminence by a lifetime of slog or a magazine of bullets, and the universal deception, willingly arrived at, that their inhabitants are in some measure recipients of a divine or at least presidential grace.

I gave myself a walking tour of the Washington embassies, and marvellously entertaining it was, being less an architectural exhibition than a display of national images. Much the most endearing building, I thought, was the Icelandic, which looks like a very comfortable boarding house in the outskirts of Reykjavik. Much the most alluring seemed to me the Turkish, which was designed in fact by the American George Totten, but speaks deliciously of hookah and seraglio, and ought to be overlooking the Golden Horn instead of the Rock Creek Parkway. The most anthropomorphic is the Yugoslav, which bears a distinct physical resemblance to Marshal Tito: the most geographic is the Canadian, which bears a distinct physical resemblance to Canada. I find it touching that the Dean of the Diplomatic Corps is the Ambassador of Nicaragua, with a population of four million: he has been in Washington for more than thirty years, and when he first presented his seals of office most of the countries now represented in that gallimaufry of mansions had not yet been invented.

Old-school loyalist that I am, of course I like the British Embassy best, and am not in the least resentful, though perhaps a *little* surprised, to hear that in these difficult times they have installed in the Ambassador's house that enervating contemporary device, air-conditioning. No wonder a Washington posting no longer qualifies for hazard pay! Still, up there in Lutyens's country house, red Sussex brick in Washington N.W., the diplomatic masque is unashamed, and English gentlemen still stand fastidious and self-amused beneath their chandeliers. When I first came to Washington, twenty years ago, that easy Oxford manner was a local cynosure. Ambitious Americans affected it, American aristocrats wore it like a uniform, Washington hostesses talked incessantly about dukely cousins or ancestral homes in Wiltshire.

Fashion is doubly fickle, though, when it partners power, and today most of the local Wasps, if they have not buzzed away altogether, have discreetly folded their wings. I met a few. I had coffee with A—, more indelibly English of accent, more unswervingly patrician of style, than any Englishman I have met for years. I renewed my acquaintance with B—, who spoke kindly of Harold Macmillan and asked what Lord Caccia was doing these days. I ran into the chairman of the Episcopalian Cathedral Garden Committee, who complained about the *dreadful* mess people made with Coca-Cola cans, conjured her dog Flicker to obey the garden regulations, and begged me not to notice the weeds. I met a retired colonel who mentioned the Philadelphia Morrises and told me to look out for an interesting essay he had contributed to the journal of the Daughters of the American Revolution. But gone, or at least adeptly modified, are the Anglophile enthusiasms which, only a generation ago, so largely set the social tone of the city. For better or worse, America has found itself since then, and the pretensions are home-grown now.

An ambassador nevertheless, as Sir Henry Wotton wrote, is a man sent abroad to lie for his country, and in every one of those plushy embassies, turreted or curtain-walled, rich in monarchic symbols or austere with socialist dogma, the envoys are doing their best to sustain their own deceptions. I went to the British Embassy one evening to see the pianist Vladimir Horowitz presented with the Gold Medal of the Royal Philharmonic Society, brought to him on a cushion by a marvellously suave young Secretary, and handed over with a graceful ambassadorial speech about violent times and the meaning of art. Mr. Horowitz seemed pleased, but instead of replying in kind sat down at the piano and played in a highly vibrant and indeed imperial manner 'God Save The Queen', making full use of the sustaining pedal.

There was a pause at the end of it, and instantly, as the last notes faded, I clicked the scene in my memory: and so I have held it there like a flash from a dream, the Ambassador benignly at attention, the young diplomats rigid all about, the American guests clutching their champagne glasses, the great room aglow with carpets and portraits, the pianist's hand raised in a last grandiloquence—an ornate little vignette of Washington, where life so often shimmers through a gauze curtain, insubstantially.

*   *   *

Often time itself seems suspended in Washington. Superficially the current American mutations show, from floppy moustaches at the Washington *Post* to mock folk-art on the Georgetown sidewalks. Physically few cities have changed more radically in a lifetime: there are cab-drivers still on the road who remember the building of the

Lincoln Memorial, let alone the Jefferson, and a city which fifty years ago was no more than an appendage to the Capitol is now a huge metropolis in its own right. Yet in the political heart of it, though the Presidents come and go, though the administrative style allegedly changes and the stance of government shifts, still the essence seems to stay the same. I was taken to lunch one day to a restaurant political people favour, and looking around at the other tables, seemed to see there precisely the same sober-tied lobbyists, identically the same smiling Congressmen, with just the same haircuts and almost the same suits, as I had seen there eating unquestionably the same rockfish twenty years before.

They were *not* the same men. If I could see them side by side with their predecessors of 1954, I would doubtless notice differences of manner, dress, even bone-structures perhaps. But set against the monumental presence of government, like mutes in a mausoleum they assumed a common identity. In Georgetown especially, which is, I suppose, the most obsessively political residential enclave in the world, an extraordinary sense of sameness sometimes overcomes me. Georgetown is an innocent exterior disguising an immensely worldly, not to say tigerish community. Most of its houses are poky, inconvenient and unbeautiful, but a sort of rich inner glue of common interest and influence has permeated them, sticking them together through cracks in the brickwork, and making many of them feel less like individual houses than wings of some awkwardly dismembered mansion. Outside, too, their often undistinguished fronts have been successfully disguised with foliage, shutters and colonial lamps, giving the whole district so powerful a sense of unity that its streets have become more or less interchangeable, and I came to feel that if I got the address confused, and went to the wrong house for dinner, nobody would notice anyway.

There are spontaneous parts of Georgetown, modest parts too, but the dominant characteristic of the quarter is a rich premeditation. Good taste is everywhere: original style, not often. Georgetown's culture is the culture of politics, is all in the game. It flows watchfully with the tide, abstract to pop, kinetic to representational, *Time* one year to *Rolling Stone* the next. I doubt if there are, for instance, just at the moment anyway, many Victorian narrative pictures in the Georgetown drawing-rooms; I wonder how often Mendelssohn, for example, is played on the Georgetown hi-fis; I doubt if, let us say, Somerset Maugham is prominently displayed in many Georgetown bookcases. Washington taste is rather like Washington ambition: politic.

Within the cramped opulence of the Georgetown setting, which is a kind of lush mirror-image of the Capitol scene, the faces of the Washington activists are shaded still further into anonymity, lost among their peers and followers, so that even the affection of marriage, parenthood or friendship seems to lose its truth. It is like a shadow-world. At one Georgetown dinner I was introduced to a man I seemed to think I knew. Had I met him in Europe somewhere? Was he a colleague from the distant past? Or was he, as so often happens these days, not a personal acquaintance at all, but an actor from a television serial whose face is familiar to us all? He seemed a nice man, and I did not like to hurt his feelings by admitting that I had forgotten what show I had seen him in, but I did venture to ask what was the name again. 'George McGovern,' I was told.

Ah yes.

*   *   *

The ultimate self-deception is the deception of permanence, and Heaven knows this is not unique to Washington. Every empire has assumed its own eternity: within a decade of each other both Churchill and Hitler spoke of their respective empires lasting a thousand years apiece. I am sure there are many people in Washington who have envisaged their capital destroyed by a nuclear missile, a fate for which it seems almost expressly designed, but I suspect there are few politicians who see their ambitions, their successes and their professional sorrows merely as transient contributions to decay. It seems so important, no doubt, when your name goes on that door at last; it seems so desperate, when you lose that election; it seems so magic a moment, when the House Majority Leader recognizes you in the elevator, or the Washington *Post* profiles you, or you get that job on the senatorial staff or the committee pay-roll. It is all a parade! Nowhere in the world, I think, do people take themselves more seriously than they do in Washington, or seem so indifferent to other perceptions than their own. Whether they are granite reactionaries or raging revolutionaries, they find it hard to see beyond.

As a corrective to this most fundamental error, I used sometimes to go and sit on the grass beside the Mall, where the tourist coaches stop beside the great round pool below Grant's statue, and the white mass of the Capitol looms portentously above it all. I am a cultist of the *genii loci*, those misty and marvellous spirits which are, I believe, literally conjured into being by the force of human experience: and though the Capitol is not very old by mystic standards, still there can be few buildings on earth more compelling to such sprites, so that on the right day I could almost see their vaporous trails circling the great dome, or intercepting each other with comic gestures above the crowning figure of freedom (for they know better than any of us how little liberty has to do with politics). The thought of them there, and the high intentions which had for nearly two centuries attended that site, awed me rather, and when I found the ground a little dusty there, and cast around for something to sit on, for a moment I really wondered if it would be improper to place my bottom on a map of central Washington.

The point about the *genii loci*, though, is that they outlive their creators. I could not easily imagine Washington actually deserted, but as I sat there in the hot sun I did not find it hard to imagine the city past its heyday. There is an Indian feeling to Washington on a hot fall day, when the grass is browned by the long summer, the trees have lost their flowers, and the taxis are bouncing desolately through the dust of the new subway excavations—a slight sense of Calcutta, say, where the monuments of another greatness look out forlornly across the parched Maidan. Then I saw Washington, too, frayed in decline: the gleaming white of the Capitol grey and fretted, the pool blotched with scum, cherry trees dead in their twos and threes, litter blowing across the grass and slogans scrawled on the statue's plinth. Then I saw the remaining spaces of the Washington plan filled in not with ostentatious halls and galleries, but with the cheap jerry-buildings of an impoverished bureaucracy, and I saw potholes in those ceremonial boulevards, and beggars sleeping disregarded in the shade of the Washington Monument, and two or three mangy dogs nosing about the rubbish outside the U.S. Court House.

But as I sat engrossed in this melancholy fancy, I heard a camera click. 'Thanks, ma'am,' said the cheerful young man with his girl, and instantly I remembered that illusion is a prism: for to them, who was I but your perennial Washington tourist, from Iowa or from Arkansas, sitting on her guide-map to keep her skirt clean, a history teacher perhaps, or a realtor's wife of artistic yearnings, sketching the Capitol in her notebook, recording patriotic emotions, or resolving once more to keep America beautiful in a mental as well as a physical sense?

*   *   *

The elder statesman, being rather deaf, had to lean over the sofa to conduct the conversation, but was not deterred. 'Who's that? What? Sure, I remember when Jack cut off aid there. Sam didn't agree. Ted did. De Gaulle didn't want it. I thought we should. What? Who's that? Sure, I remember that very well—the Bay of Pigs—the U-2—Eisenhower didn't have any idea—Khrushchev didn't know—Sam said yes—Dulles said no—I told the Committee it couldn't be done. When? Who d'you say? Sure, some people say it was the Truman Doctrine, but it wasn't, only Jack/Sam/Johnson/Harry said look, if we don't get there as sure as hell there'll be trouble with Nasser/Chiang/Nehru/Thieu. Which? When d'you say? Sure, I met him that evening. Macmillan was there, Gromyko was there, Winston was there, Stalin was there, Napoleon said look, Gladstone said wait a minute, Robert E. Lee was there, Lincoln said to me, I said to the Kaiser, Metternich said not on your sweet life, Bismarck walked out, he was a very difficult guy to deal with. . . . What's that? Which? Sure, yes, I'd love some, no sugar thanks. . . .'

For, of course, there is to the gigantic fantasy of Washington a hardly less enormous element of truth. If I have romanticized that monologue towards the end, I have not distorted its message—which is that like it or not, Washington is the summit of the western world. The great seldom seem so great when one meets them face to face, and in Washington especially they seem to shrink in the flesh—the only man I saw in the city who struck me at once with the magic of leadership was the cantor or precentor of a group of Hari Krishna devotees I came across one day on the Georgetown sidewalk. Nevertheless, the names that Washington so loves to drop really are the names that will survive in the history books, and that elder statesman across the sofa was truly reminiscing about the stuff of legend. His wife was there too, and her conversation was hardly less Pepysian or Nicolsonian. 'I do think,' she said '—and I've just this minute run into him at the reception for President Ganfoni—I really do think Henry's getting a *little* too fat.'

In one whose sense of history is sceptical, even condescending, this kind of small talk raises more a giggle than a gasp: but I pulled myself together whenever I could, and reminded myself that in Washington more than anywhere, perhaps, the great game of politics is played for human lives and happiness. So powerful is the pageant of Washington, so compelling I can well see is the fascination of its charades, that it takes a conscious effort of the will to translate its illusions into reality.

There is a car that drives around the streets towing a coffin inscribed
with the text 'The Death of Philippine Democracy'. In a city accustomed to the comings and goings of Immortals, such a little cortège
goes unremarked. I obliged myself, though, when it passed me one
day, to wonder just what it meant, and what tenuous chain of appeal
it represented. At one end of the demonstration stood the White
House, the fount of all mercy, whose incumbent was commonly
supposed to have achieved office by a dubious deal with his predecessor, a common crook, but who would one day be honoured in
this city, no doubt, whatever his shortcomings, with a Memorial
Grove, Archive or Sculpture Garden. At the other end of the message
lay—what? Men in prison? Wives distraught? The knock at the midnight door? I did not, to be honest, know much about the state of
Philippine democracy, but just to speculate about the connection,
between the state of human happiness in the Manila backstreets, and
the condition of human power in the Oval Office, was a useful
exercise in perspectives.

Here is another. I shared a taxi into town one day with a lady in a
blue silk turban, who was visiting Washington and was about to meet
her daughter for lunch at a Hot Shoppe. Down the great thoroughfares we drove, and all the memorials of the American splendour
passed us one by one, granite and concrete, obelisk and colonnade.
My companion drew my attention now and then to a White House
or a Treasury, but it was as we passed the Capitol itself, and were
deploring the state of the world in general, that she spoke the words
I best remember: 'I sometimes wonder oh, what kind of a world are
we bringing our children into, when you have to pay a quarter for a
doughnut?'

Twenty-five cents for a doughnut! Even Americans bleed.

*   *   *

Even Washingtonians. Even Georgetownees. Even White Householders. In Washington there are many reminders, even now, of the
old American instinct towards simplicity. I was delighted to find that
a fairly ordinary-looking boat moored down at the Navy Yard, which
I took to be a lighthouse tender, perhaps, was in fact the Presidential
yacht *Sequoia*, a far cry indeed from the gilded private liners of the
European monarchies. Even the White House itself is a happy antidote,
for though Jefferson thought it big enough for a couple of Emperors,
a Pope and a Grand Lama of Tibet, by the standards of princely

mansions it is a fairly modest house, a house where, it seems to me, a family could decently and happily live, browsing through the library (or rather the Learning Resources Center), pottering through the garden, or sitting on the lawn with long cool drinks watching the Filipino caskets go by.

For there is, of course, an ordinary, human side to Washington life, deeply buried though it often seems. The shambled districts that I remember south-west of the Capitol have all been swept away, indeed, and replaced by Plazas, Malls and Award-Winning Developments, but there are still wide districts of Washington, even inner Washington, that feel like parts of a real city, immune to the central contagion. On 7th Street S.E., within sight of the Capitol, genial butchers still offer crackling and home-made sausages beneath the shabby high-ribbed roof of the Eastern Market (even if, beside the fruiterers, the Washington Consort *does* advertise its forthcoming performance of Early Seventeenth-Century Flemish Madrigals). On K Street N.W., beneath the Whitehurst Freeway, the freight trains rumble among the waterside cobbles for all the world as though Georgetown were still the little river port of its origins (even if Rive Gauche, just a block away, *does* charge eleven dollars without tax for a straight *filet mignon*). At Fort McNair, within the dire shadow of the War College, a most agreeable row of early Victorian villas stands beside the Washington Channel, white and wholesome, like village houses around a green. Even in the central shopping streets I sometimes feel myself to be, not in the capital of the western world, but in some characteristic small city of the south, blistered with heat, where politics aims no further than the next Mayor and Sheriff, and there is nowhere to go on Sunday but church, the drug store or the evangelist's tent outside of town.

The rich and the poor, transcending politics, do exist in Washington, and often seem equally immune to its deceptions. To the very, very rich the ambitions of Capitol Hill can seem trivial or peripheral: 'What do you want most in the world?' Mr. Joe Hirshhorn was asked, on the night the vast Hirshhorn Gallery was opened in the very heart of monumental Washington. 'Money,' he replied. Hardly a stone's throw away, closer still to the Capitol, I remarked to a hot-dog vendor one day what a fantastic place it was to have a stand. 'Sure is,' he agreed, 'fantastic up till Labor Day anyways, sixty or seventy dollars in a single morning. . . .' 'Garbage is garbage like any place else,' said the refuse collector when I asked him if he ever found secret

documents in the litter bins. 'I wouldn't know a secret document if I
saw one.'

Such earthy truisms mean more in Washington. For myself I long
ago concluded that generally speaking the only important part of life
is the private part, and that public ambition is seldom worth the
cherishing. This, of course, disqualifies me from participation in
Washington's affairs, but at least it makes me a detached observer.
So I tried hard, during my stay in the city, to flake away the surface
of the civic conduct and reach the substance beneath: and if I often
found that surface and substance were indistinguishable, sure enough
often I managed to penetrate the display, to find a homely aphorism
or a twenty-five-cent doughnut beneath. Even in Washington, D.C.
all is relative. 'Nothing alters life so absolutely', I overheard a woman
saying at Billy Martin's Carriage House, 'as having your ears pierced.'

*   *   *

'I'll take you', said a kind friend after lunch, 'to the *real* Washington.'
He has a piquant humour, and I rather hoped that in this all too
familiar threat he was referring to the Wax Museum. But no, instead
he took me up 14th Street to show me the gaps and parking lots
created in the race riots of 1968, and back via T Street, where one or
two black prostitutes, blinking uncomfortably in the harsh light of
afternoon, hung unhopefully around the street corners.

An inescapable reality of Washington is its blackness. When I first
came to the city it somehow did not show. Today it is all-intrusive,
and one can hardly miss its underlying conflicts. Old-fashioned phrases
like 'Get out of the way you damn nigger', or 'Don't blow your horn
at me, you shit', mingle hourly with the monumental texts: in no
American city, at least in the past five years, have I felt the old anti-
pathies so viciously. This is partly because the District of Columbia is
still, in a political sense, hardly more than a ward of Congress—a black
plantation around the Hill. And it is partly because it is neither exactly
a southern city, nor a northern, so that two inherited sets of mores
clash here, leaving everyone uncertain. I read somewhere that Washington, a city of some 750,000 people, is now the largest black city
outside Africa: and for my taste much of its real elegance, most of its
true originality, springs from its black awareness. If I want to know
the way in Washington, I try to ask a black: for I like the directness
of the response I am likely to get, the flash, the style of it.

I looked in one evening at a posh black function at the Washington

Hilton, and was greeted with a brilliance that made the poor George-town socialites seem dowdy. What terrific strapping women! What gorgeous ruffled shirts! How quick the smiles and explosive the laughter! What energy! What self-esteem! In downtown Washington the fury of blackness expresses itself often in violence, and there is probably no city in the world more thickly policed than Washington, where every street seems to have its prowling patrol car, and the air is meshed with howls, blurps and radio signals. In the upper echelons of black society, though, that fury expresses itself in very different, more formidable terms, and brings back to Washington a reality that possesses, I like to think, some of the original American excitement. (Though, of course, it is only *half*-black, the American Negro having interbred so frequently with whites and Indians, and one of the lesser ironies of the place is the attitude of the African students at Howard University, who view the junketings of Washington black society with a distinctly mordant eye.)

I went to the House of Representatives to attend the celebrations of the 200th anniversary of the First Continental Congress. The ceremony did not at first impress me, for there is nothing so flaccid as American pageantry. The Congressmen looked pasty, as though most of them needed a good night's sleep, or some fresh vegetables for a change. The drum and fife band, in wigs and redcoats, looked downright silly. The representatives who read a fraternal message from the Senate were inaudible. The potted palms they had stacked around the Speaker's desk made the Chamber look like the setting for a tea dance long ago.

Presently, though, when the band had played its opening piece, the chairman had spoken his introduction, and I was beginning to doodle, a very unexpected voice broke the spell. It was a rich, clever voice, reading with great skill and intensity a passage from Jefferson—'Mr. Jefferson', as he is still apparently known in these parts, as Mr. Rhodes is remembered in Africa. I looked up from my notebook then, and turned my attention to the speaker. She was a youngish, stoutish, very vigorous-looking black woman, whose very posture on the rostrum seemed to express a combination of defiance and resolution, and made everybody else look flabby. I left after her speech, for I thought the academics billed to follow her might be bathetic by contrast, and I am glad I did: I had never heard before of Barbara Jordan (D., Houston), but of all the politicians I saw in Washington, she was the one I am least likely to forget.

* * *

She was not the only woman, either, who seemed to me to bring an emphatic new distinction to Washington life. Women have changed in most places, of course, in the past twenty years, but nowhere more radically or more significantly than they have in Washington, D.C. When I first came to the city the feminist movement was, so to speak, in abeyance, its theoretical political objectives achieved, its practical social targets not yet formulated. Political women in those days were not generally attractive. There were women in Congress, of course, but Washington was still in the hand-that-rocks-the-cradle era, or more pertinently, the hand-that-makes-the-table-arrangement phase. The Monstrous Regiment marched still. I remember vividly my first Washington hostesses when, young and terribly British myself, I arrived with unimpeachable letters of introduction and found myself swirled into the Georgetown vortex. Thickly made up and diligently fashionable they greeted me then, and their skirts were precisely the Paris length, and they celebrated their importance in diamonds and pearls, and stood graciously at the senatorial side, inexorably pursuing their husbands' interests.

They survive, and have grown yet more gracious and even more diamondal with the passage of the years, but far more impressive nowadays is the new Washington breed of free women, to be found in every rank or station. I hope I am not biased in admiring them so. I hope I am not naïve, either, for I do see that in the course of their progress towards what I myself take to be the evolutionary goal of androgyny, they may retrogress sometimes, or pick up bad habits from the old hands. But for the moment anyway they seem to me the most trustworthy people in Washington, the people who see life in its truest perspective, the people whose opinions I most valued, whose advice I most welcomed, and whose explanations of the American electoral system I found most nearly comprehensible.

Having newly realized their own potential in this most male-dominated of western cities, they have the frankness of confidence: they are comrades still, the best of them, one with another, and they are genuinely inspired more by principles than by profits. Also the Washington game is more immediate for them: they are not only the players now, only yesterday they were the pawns. It is a grand and moving phenomenon, I think, here in the old shrine of individualism, to see one half of humanity coming into its own at last, on a plane of intention and sensibility far beyond the theatricals of Women's Lib.

But, of course, I *am* biased. I believe the traditional feminine principles of gentleness, loyalty and realism to be the best ones for politics: here in Washington today, combined as they now can be with power and opportunity, I believe them to be the hope of the world.

*　　*　　*

It occurred to me one day that Washington seemed to go to bed rather early. When I asked why, I was told that it was partly because the streets were unsafe at night, but partly because so many Washingtonians were *émigrés* from the country, used to getting up at six to milk the cows, spread the muck, cut the cane or open up the corner store. I liked this romantic explanation, without much believing in it, and certainly the pretensions of Washington are often redeemed by a small town, even a country feeling. The Washington *Post*, the premier political newspaper of America, descends very rapidly from the high politics of its editorials through the antics of its society news to the neighbourly gossip of its obituaries—'Long Time Resident, 90, Retired Painter' or 'Aide At Library Here'.

There *is* a kind of family charm to the presence in the capital of all those provincial politicians. I love to see them ushering constituents around the Capitol, benign and avuncular, and to observe the endearing combination of the condescending (for they are after all Elected Representatives of the People) and the wheedling (for they do after all need votes) with which they shook hands with their respectful visitors at the end of the tour—'We sure are obliged to you, Senator'— 'We certainly are, Sir'—'I shall never forget this day, Senator'—'*Fine, just fine, great to have you along . . . .*' Meeting a likely looking gent in a Capitol corridor, I tried a gambit myself, as a speculation. 'Morning, Senator,' I said. 'Hullo there young lady,' he instantly replied. 'Having fun?'—and off he strode to his office, chumping, alas for my purposes, not an actual, but at least a metaphysical cigar.

There are two big Washington airports. From the lovely Dulles Airport the international flights leave, and some people find it exciting to watch them taking off for Rio or Frankfurt, London or Dakar. I much prefer the lesser allegory of the National Airport, beyond the Arlington Cemetery. When L'Enfant laid out Washington he conceived it as a series of hubs from which symbolic highways would radiate not merely across the capital, I suppose, but far across the nation too—just as Washington's original highway, the Potomac, took the traders past the Georgetown wharfs into the Appalachian hinterland. A much more telling hub now, though, is that airport: nothing is more exciting in Washington than to watch the jets come in from the far corners of America, from the States with the magical names, from the prairie clusters and the California sprawl, from all the huge body of America to this, the marble heart of it. Washington sophisticates tend to scoff, when I express this lyric pleasure to them: but there, I like that sort of thing.

*   *   *

Another thing I like is the disrespect which survives the institutionalization of Washington. I do not mean the specific disrespect of broadsheet, posters or black comedy: I mean the older, deeper disrespect for pomp and circumstance in general, which used to be, for half the world, the very meaning of this republic. One tends to forget the flow of this ancient current, I must say, when the Presidential caravan sweeps out of the White House with its cohorts of policemen and bulging bodyguards, but in a way it is what Watergate was all about, and it is not dry yet. 'Yeah,' said a woman loudly and complacently, stepping back from a china cabinet during our tour of the White House—'Chipped!' The apotheosis of the Presidency proceeds apace, despite the heresies of Watergate, but in Washington one still sometimes feels the old republican instincts.

The most appealing part of this, for the stranger, is the railway-station feeling of Congress itself. I love to wander around its corridors, and contrast its cheerful informality with the stately self-esteem of lesser assemblies. What fun to ride in the subway train from one side to the other, ruffled in the sub-Capitolian breeze, while the train driver reads his paperback thriller backwards and forwards through the legislature! What a laugh to add your contribution to the rest room graffiti—Cindy loves Ron, or Happyness Is Elvis! How happily improbable, to be eating your bean soup in the basement of Congress! Of all the national Parliaments I have ever visited, only one rivals the jollity of Capitol Hill, and that is the National Assembly at Reykjavik, where the page boys in jeans and sweaters will run out and get you a bag of chips, if you ask them nicely.

*   *   *

So the realities assert themselves, and we are brought to the core of Washington. The most fascinating aspect of Washington, the fire of it, is the fusion between what is false, what is all too real and what is hallucinatory. Balance is the point of Washington—between rulers

and ruled, between the three branches of Government, between the
affairs of the world and the death of 'Local Resident, 90', between
what is magnificent in the American idea, and what is despicable in
the American practice. It is the perpetual juggling of antitheses that
gives the city an excitement far beyond its architecture, and makes
every day in Washington, if scarcely a festival, at least an event.

At the end of 1974 the city was in the aftermath of nightmare, and
was still only half-wakened from it. Often when one emerges from a
particularly ghastly and convincing dream, it is at once a relief and a
perverse delight to re-enact its details in the mind—even to embellish
them, if you are of an inventive turn. Washington was doing this then.
Its people did not realize that, though the whole world had, like a
solicitous friend attending an acid trip, observed its ordeal from the
outside, only in Washington was the hideous dream an immediate
personal experience. They were, to be frank, a bit boring about
Watergate. They mulled it over and over, re-living all its Gothic
thrills: perhaps the real world felt anti-climactic to them, and they
half wished they were back in the frightful limbo of the night before.

I was startled by this phenomenon. I had supposed that, with Nixon
gone and his accomplices discredited, Washington would be settling
with relief into a more composed routine. I expected a contemplative,
if shaken community: I found instead a nest of zealots. There was a
venom still in the air, something more poisonous I thought than mere
political reaction, something savage and paranoic. I had experienced
moments of political trauma before—the McCarthy hearings in this
same city, the Suez débacle in Britain, France's abdication among the
colons of Algeria—but I had never felt quite so insidious a sense of shock
and repulsion as I felt in Washington then. I ventured sometimes,
foolishly, to express some of my soppier inbred prejudices, like forgiving and forgetting, or making a fresh start, but I soon discovered
that just at that moment the liberal ethic was hardly at a premium in
Washington. Gentle and civilized old friends of mine declared not
merely that they despised and resented Nixon, but that they *hated* him.
One could only compare him, said one respected commentator, to a
hyena. 'I don't know about these Nixons,' a hotel porter said to me.
'If you cut them, would blood come out?' 'I'd sooner pardon that
guy', somebody else told me, 'than I'd pardon a rattle-snake.'

Slowly I grew to differentiate these various responses, and to
commiserate with some of them, for I recognize this particular nightmare to have been true. What I found more disturbing was the

popular feeling of a general betrayal, expressed so often in Washington through the myth of conspiracy. The conspiratorial strain, like the violent strain, has figured largely in the American past, not least because it has so often been founded upon hard fact. The Elders of Zion may be imaginary, but the Mafia distinctly is not, and the present taste for things eerie and unexplained has given extra force to the sense that evil and secret energies are webbed beneath the surface of political life. Sometimes my informants specialized in single conspiracies: sometimes they apparently lumped together all the tragedies of the 1960s and 1970s, all the scandals and assassinations, the cover-ups and the revelations, the wars and even the illnesses in one hazed but embittered conception. Johnson had Kennedy murdered, Nixon had Wallace shot, Connolly was behind it all, Mitchell was only a front, Ford was in it, Liddy was at Dallas, Calley knew Haldeman, Ruby was a classmate of Dean—'Did you ever stop to think about this: why did McGovern choose Eagleton in the first place? You think he did not know about that guy's head-shrink? *Sure he knew . . . .*'

On a higher level this instinct turns into a conviction that *everyone* has something to hide, an unfortunate conviction in political terms, for it is undeniably true. Faith in analysis is strong in America, and the notion that some truths are best left fallow is not popular in the capital. I was at a dinner table one night when one of the investigative reporters who were the contemporary lions of Washington was discussing new targets—Kissinger, Ford, Rockefeller, nobody had ever *really* done Rocky . . . I found it a depressing conversation. Who was there, I bleakly asked, what single leader, to whom they could give their loyalty and trust, without sensing the need for an exposé? But answer came there none, for they had changed the subject by then, and over a particularly delicious and innovative sole with orange sauce, were back to Watergate once more.

*   *   *

There is no denying the stimulation of this extraordinary *mise en scène*, where truth and innuendo, fact and legend are all intermingled. It is like a political Hollywood: faces familiar to the world are the commonplaces of its sidewalks, and the tour buses take their sightseers to Watergate precisely as they tour the Homes of the Stars—as my Washington guide-book says, there is no better place than the Army and Navy Club 'to catch a glimpse of high-ranking officers off duty'. The Washington actors are perpetually on-stage, and their audience is half-drawn into the performance, so that the sense of theatre binds every aspect of the city together, and makes it difficult even for visiting hedonists to remain altogether detached. Even I expressed a political opinion once or twice in Washington, and nearly always found it, whether it expressed the reactionary or the radical in me, Welsh intuition or English decadence, instantly and conclusively squelched. Coals are hard to sell, in Newcastle.

I went to the opening of the Watergate cover-up trial, when Messrs. Mitchell, Haldeman *et al.* appeared before Judge Sirica in the U.S. Court House. During the lunch recess I found myself descending the court-room stairs behind John Ehrlichman, who courteously opened the door for me before passing with his wife into the sunshine of Constitution Avenue. Against all my better instincts, for in me the urges of an investigative reporter are not simply atrophied, they are actually reversed, I decided to follow the couple down the avenue, and see where they went. At first a small pack of photographers pursued them like seagulls following a trawler, dismissing them at a street corner with genial insincerities—'Thanks a lot', 'Take care', 'Have a good lunch.' Then they were all alone, and in the bright sunshine they walked hand in hand towards the Federal Triangle.

Nobody looked twice at them. Nobody noticed them, so far as I could tell. Not a secretary nudged her companion as they passed, not a hard-hat stared from the subway works. Ehrlichman's name and face were familiar wherever newspapers are read: he was standing trial for one of the most shattering political crimes of the century: only a few weeks before he had been one of the most powerful men in America: he had been called the Goering to Nixon's Hitler, the jackal perhaps to the hyena. Yet nobody noticed. I was oddly touched, sentimentalist that I am, by the sight of that fated couple waiting for the traffic lights to change, and felt a momentary urge to reach out to them, however sinister his designs, with a smile or a touch of the sleeve: but I restrained myself, and presently they crossed the Mall, still hand in hand, and disappeared for their half hour of privacy into the National Gallery of Art. ('You think they didn't know you was watching? *Sure they knew . . . .*')

'He was a bad, bad man,' my friends told me reprovingly, when I confessed to this little episode. Hand in hand, they said, was the oldest cliché in the game. Heart's no use without head, they said. Mercy demands justice, they told me. Well, I know it, and it is a chill fact about the Washington theatre that the villains up there are not acting.

Here the melodrama is true. That really is the Pentagon scowling beyond the river. Ring 351-1100 and the nasal bored voice of the operator really will announce 'Central Intelligence'. This is the city of the wiretap and the bodyguard and the foreign spy, where assassination is a daily possibility, where the Pentagon disposes its missiles and the Navy Department its submarines. Here in Washington indeed, just down the road from my hotel, is the black box which, at a word from the White House, can effectively destroy the world. There's *grand guignol* for you!

Capital of a violent nation, Washington is accustomed to violent values. Its general air is easy-going, but its bad men are truly bad, and brute force lies always near the heart of it. The climax of the public tour of the F.B.I. headquarters, in the Federal Triangle, is a demonstration shoot by a marksman, who shuts himself in a glass-walled range, muffles his ears with a head-set, and shoots at a paper target in the shape of a human torso, first with a revolver, then with a submachine-gun. He was using demonstration bullets actually, our guide explained when I attended this display, to make a cleaner hole: the ones they used in real life ripped the target about a little, so you couldn't tell how accurately they shot. Our marksman that day, an amiable man who looked like a dentist, perhaps, or a bank teller approaching retirement, shot very accurately indeed, placing all his bullets within what we were told was the most desirable area, around the heart and lungs; and soon, opening his glass door and pressing a button, he brought his torso-target winging spookily and suggestively back towards us on a runner—'Like I say,' our guide repeated, 'in real life it'd be more torn about.' In the kindliest way the agent removed it from its fastening and folded it into a tidy package: and looking around his smiling and grateful audience, and choosing the smallest infant in the front row, with a quip about playing hooky from school that day he presented him with the mangled evidence of his skill. 'Real neat,' his mother thought it: the tour is, so they told me at the gate, one of the most popular experiences the Nation's Capital has to offer.

If there is something infantile to all these dramatics, the bombs, the wiretaps, the F.B.I. *machismo*, well, there is something juvenile of course to the whole paraphernalia of power, wherever it is pursued. (The only wholly adult statesman I have ever heard of was Lord Salisbury, who once said that his notion of British foreign policy was to drift gently downstream, now and then putting an oar out to prevent a collision.) In Washington the silliness of it is only intensified by the volatility of America itself, which seems to me at once the genius and the absurdity of the republic. America is the land of the instant flattery, the absolute rejection. Here more than anywhere fashions shift, and opinion follows its leaders of the day. Where are the protesters of yesteryear? Where are the McCarthyites of the decade before? A cause vanishes, and so does its fervour; an issue arises, and there are convictions to match. A single New York critic can destroy a play: a single Washington columnist can destroy a reputation: a nation which votes a man into office by an overwhelming majority in 1972 can discover him to be a common criminal by 1974. The American pendulum, whose pivot is in Washington, swings not simply side to side, but erratically backwards and forwards too.

It seldom, though, goes round in circles. It is hard to be bored in Washington. The scandals are always fresh. New every morning breaks the excitement. Nothing is ordinary. The moment I left the trail of the Ehrlichmans that day, I encountered another familiar of the Washington scene, equally ignored by the lunchtime crowds. He was a very serious-looking man of Jewish cast, dressed entirely as President Lincoln and walking purposefully in the direction of the White House—where else? He carried a briefcase under his arm, inscribed, so far as I could without rudeness make out, with the name Abraham B. Lincoln: and this was satisfyingly puzzling, in a city of cryptic mysteries, for as every loyal citizen knows, Abe Lincoln has no middle name.

*   *   *

A hallucinatory quality is part of modern American life. It goes with space travel, with electronics, with drugs, with contemporary art, with the knowledge always at the backs of our minds, especially in Washington, D.C., that we have the power to blow the world up. The nature of reality has shifted too, so that illusion has acquired new substance, and neither space, nor time, nor matter can lightly be defined (let alone truth).

So the delusions of Washington, if they are delusions, are the delusions of America: just as America's own faults and merits are, in a less intense or underdeveloped degree, common to us all. One reads constantly that the American public is pining for a thorough reform of political life, an end to corruption in high places. But the corruption which, as the story of Nixon revealed, is endemic to Washington, is different only in application, not in kind, from the general mayhem.

What Nixon represented in detail, Washington admirably illustrates in panorama. The big lie is only the small lie magnified, and I suspect it to be the only true political aphorism, that a nation gets the leaders it deserves. What is F.B.I. surveillance but investigative reporting from the other side? Who in Washington has not bugged, if not another's private telephone, at least another's private business? White House double-speak is only the old Georgetown flattery, employed in another genre. There is only a difference of scale, not of value, between pretending to like a picture you detest, and charging the state for improvements at San Clemente.

For myself I have come reluctantly to believe that these values are inherent to democracy when it reaches a particular stage in its development—or decay: but because America does not yet share this sad persuasion, or at least prefers not to recognize it, on my last afternoon in Washington I went along to Capitol Hill to watch President Ford address a joint session of Congress about his economic policies. I suppose one might say this was the ultimate in Washington occasions— the First Citizen addressing the Legislature of his fellow countrymen, and presenting for their approval his plans for the community. At least that is how I viewed it. The thirty-eighth Presidency was another attempt, a late attempt, to prove that the system still worked, that the Washington balances made for the good of the nation—that the whole grand idea of America, so imperishably represented in Washington's images and epitaphs, was not just a sorry and discredited sham. President Ford was trying to prove that dishonesty was an American aberration, not an American norm. 'We will be good,' he seemed to be saying, like Queen Victoria before him: and the nation echoed him in the jargon of the day—*you gotta believe*!

I was not convinced about the system that afternoon, but I was convinced by President Ford. He was clearly no orator, no economist either I suspect. His speech was full of speech-writer's ham—wonderful young people—zeroing in to problems—time to intercept—pitching in with Uncle Sam. In his lapel he wore a footling ad-man's badge saying 'Win', a device he appeared fondly to suppose would soon sweep the Fifty States. When he shook hands with his old colleagues of the House, or accepted their ovation with a disarming smile, I knew as well as everyone else that the bonhomie was charged with political nuance. He was not a handsome man, nor a man of inspiration, and he had not a quarter of the magnetism of that Hari Krishna chant-leader, nor half the awful fascination of his predecessor.

Yet he stirred me. There among the ghosts and shadows, there in that great hall smoked with the fires of glory as of fraud, there in the very centre of the American meaning, he seemed to me to be doing his best. Could one ask more, in Washington, D.C.?

* * *

The object that moved me most in Washington, more than the Declaration of Independence dim-lit above its altar at the Archives, more than Grant brooding on his tall horse above the Mall, more than Giorgione's *Adoration of the Magi* (which, as a matter of fact, I do not believe to be the work of that master)—the object that most moved me was the minuscule capsule in which the first American space traveller was projected out of the earth's gravity, hunched on his pad among his dials. I looked at it for a long time on its stand at the Smithsonian, wondering at the courage that once inhabited it, and contemplating the vast pyramid of money and brains of which it was the apex. As I did so I subjected myself to another of those self-summoned visions to which I am prone, and I imagined myself leaving Washington strapped in its padded chair. Up I went with a swoosh, up through the splintered museum roof, and presently the domes and obelisks were flattened below me, and the great gardens and boulevards were retreating fast, and the Potomac was only a silver thread, and all the big radial roads were spinning, spinning through my window, and the very shape of Washington was lost in the mass of the world, and the haze of cloud, and the dim blue blur of space.

Nothing was left in my mind then but the echoes of the capital, distantly pursuing me—*Sure, I remember it well—Rocky, nobody's really done Rocky—you look terrific—that louse?—oh, what a world to bring children into—that hyena?—I mean that in a mental as well as a physical aspect—if you cut them would blood come out?—they rip the target about a little—* E Pluribus Unum—*Come to Me!—Ask Fish Bait—Twenty-five cents for a doughnut!—Sure he knew* . . . ever more faintly, ever less strident, until at last all those harsh discords were stilled into harmony, and were only another hum in the music of the spheres.

* * *

Move along lady, please. Give the kids a chance. Christ, the dumb bitch.